Physical Characteristics of the Field Spaniel

(from the American Kennel Club breed standard)

Topline: The neck slopes smoothly into the withers; the back is level, well muscled, firm and strong; the croup is short and gently rounded.

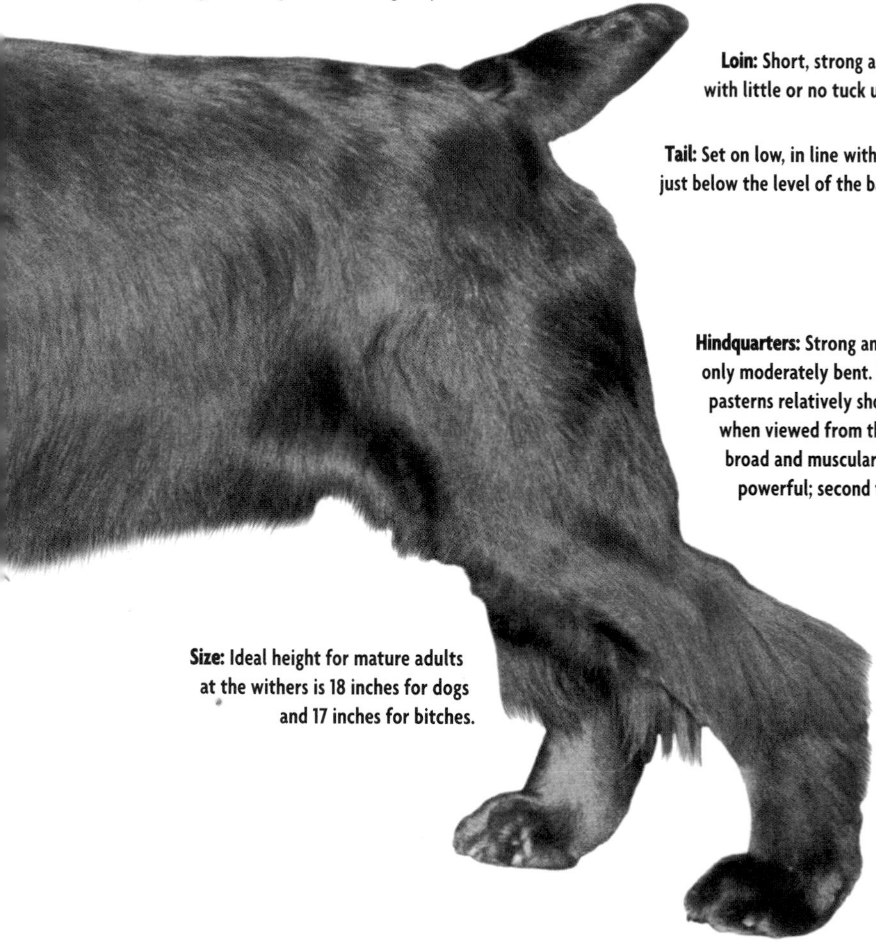

Loin: Short, strong and deep, with little or no tuck up.

Tail: Set on low, in line with the croup, just below the level of the back.

Hindquarters: Strong and driving; stifles and hocks only moderately bent. Hocks well let down; pasterns relatively short, strong and parallel when viewed from the rear. Hips moderately broad and muscular; upper thigh broad and powerful; second thigh well muscled.

Coat: Single; moderately long; flat or slightly wavy; silky; and glossy; dense and water-repellent.

Size: Ideal height for mature adults at the withers is 18 inches for dogs and 17 inches for bitches.

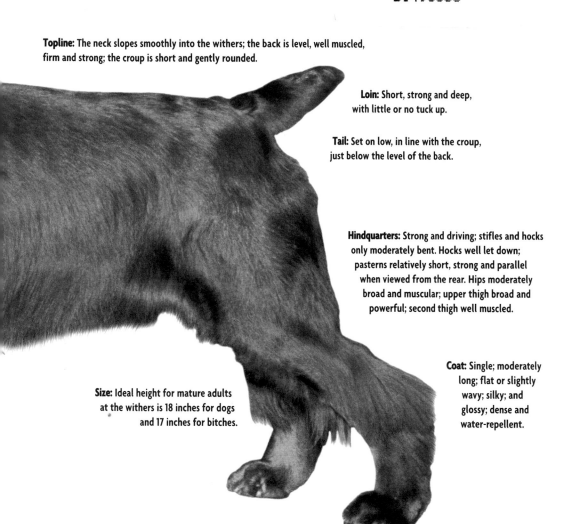

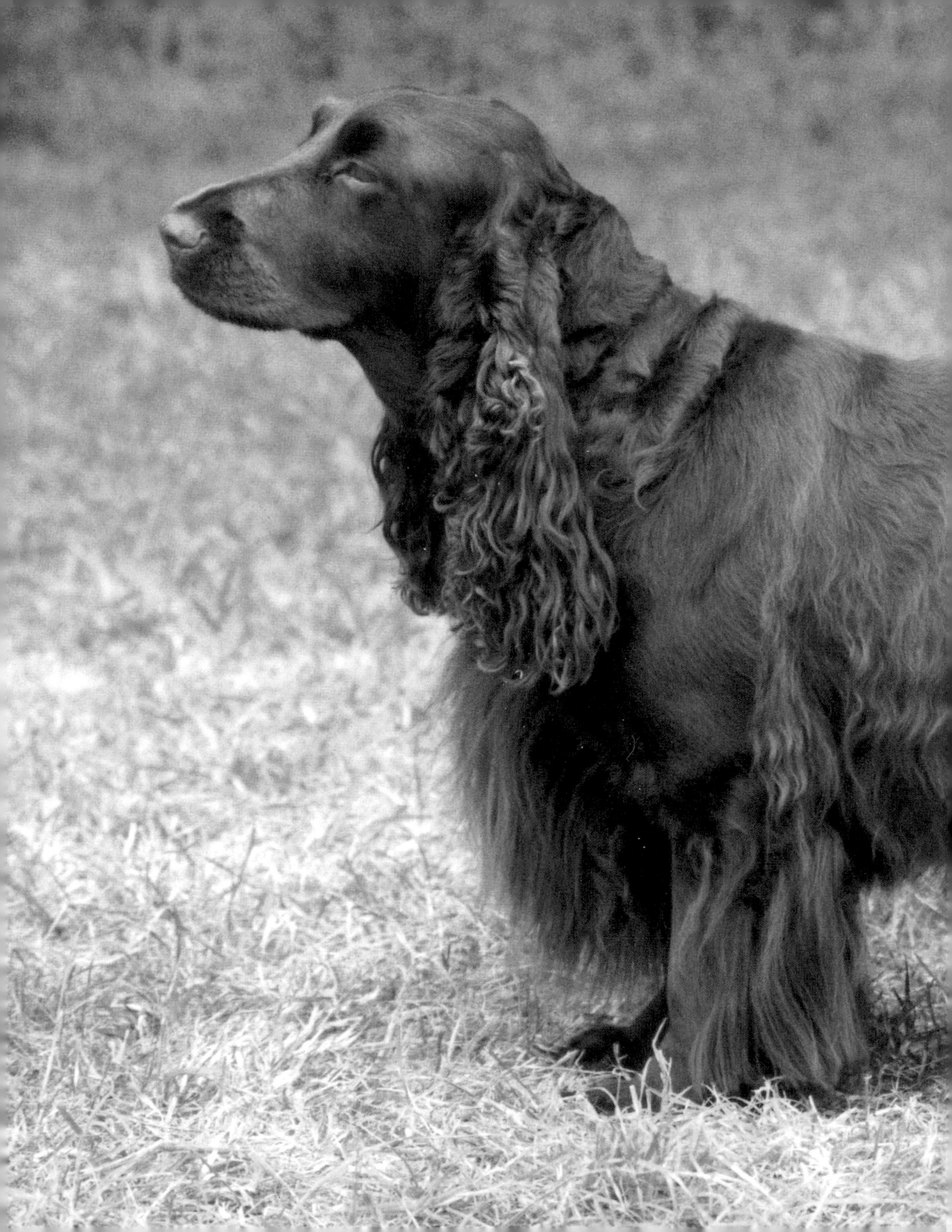

Field Spaniel

By Becki Jo Hirschy

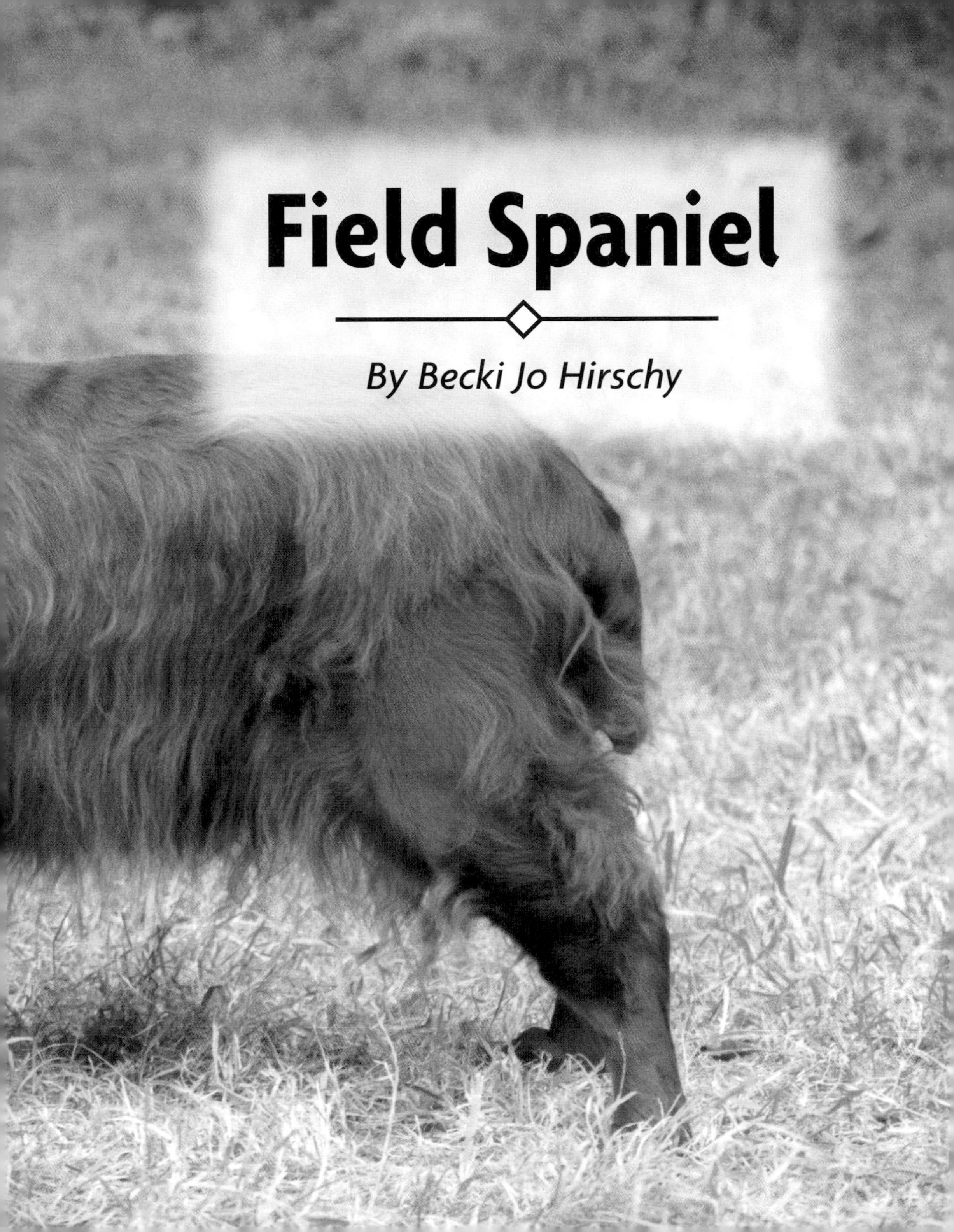

Contents

KENNEL CLUB BOOKS® **FIELD SPANIEL**
ISBN: 1-59378-291-8

308 Main Street, Allenhurst, NJ 07711 USA
Cover Design Patented: US 6,435,559 B2 • Printed in South Korea

Library of Congress Cataloging-in-Publication Data

Hirschy, Becki Jo.
Field spaniel / by Becki Jo Hirschy.
p. cm.
ISBN 1-59378-291-8
1. Field spaniel. I. Title.
SF429.F36H57 2006
636.752'4--dc22

2006011584

10 9 8 7 6 5 4 3 2 1

Photography by Carol Ann Johnson
with additional photographs by:

Norvia Behling, Booth Photography, Paulette Braun, Alan and Sandy Carey, Carolina Biological Supply, David Dalton, Isabelle Français, Kylie Hirschy, Bill Jonas, D. Kay Klein, Dr. Dennis Kunkel, Tam C. Nguyen, Phototake, Joseph Pichette, Jean Claude Revy, Steve Sherouse, Shula Shipton, Jane Swanson, Sue Thornhill, Tien Tran Photography, Otto Wahl, Lisa Winters, F. E. Wolkenheim and L. Zobel.

Illustrations by Patricia Peters.

The publisher wishes to thank all of the owners whose dogs are featured in this book, including Peter Archer, Linda Blaser, Corkie Goodell, Karen Gracz, Mrs. Hales, Becki Jo Hirschy, Kylie Hirschy, Val and Russel Mosedale, Joseph Pichette, Ed Presnall, John Sherman, Shula Shipton, Sue Thornhill and Jeffrey Zachow.

The Field Spaniel, as we know it today, originated around 1860 and has been promoted by a small but dedicated fancy. This beautiful example is Chloe, a liver and tan tracking-titled bitch.

ACKNOWLEDGMENTS

Over the past 20-plus years, a number of people have freely shared their in-depth knowledge of the Field Spaniel breed with me in candid conversation and wonderful letters: Mrs. Peggy Grayson (Westacres), Mrs. Margaret Nicholls (Lydemoor-Jonix) and Mrs. Win McCann (Pickwick), to whom I am forever grateful for my first Field, "Clara," who was allowed to come to my home in 1984. Special thanks also to Mom "Berd," sisters Jeni & Wyn, kids Jesse & Mary, Kylie & Steve and friends Janis, Karen & Tom, Jeff & Lanna, Sallys M. & H., Eric, Ed & Peggy, Arlene, Kay, Eileen, Liz, Kristy and so many more. I am forever indebted for your support.

HISTORY OF THE
FIELD SPANIEL

Although the term "Spanyell" was mentioned in literature as early as 1386, the spaniels involved in the development of the Field Spaniel date to the latter part of the 19th century. The earliest developers envisioned the Field Spaniel as a solid-black spaniel of good size and capable of active hunting. This was at odds with the preference for spaniels with patches of white in the coat. For working purposes, spaniels with patches of white were considered easier to identify when working in the field. It would be fair to ask, "If there were already plenty of spaniels to work for hunters, why was there a need for a new spaniel breed?"

One commonly held theory is that the emergence of the dog show in the 1850s may have been a reason behind the initial effort to develop the Field Spaniel in the 1860s as a separate and distinct spaniel breed. Indeed, applying a written standard to describe a perfect physical specimen may well have been a compelling reason to sort out the spaniels one from another.

History indicates that the more-or-less formal version of the dog show came into being at about the same time as the emergence of the Field Spaniel as a breed. A large, solid-black spaniel may well have been regarded as a way to win the approval of judges. Thus the Field Spaniel has often been referred to as a "manufactured" breed. A remarkable number of spaniel varieties, some now extinct as distinct breeds, were involved in the evolution of the Field Spaniel.

The modern Field Spaniel owes his foundation to dogs of unremarkable lineage, often with unremarkable names. In the early days, spaniels were often classified as either "land" or "water"

HISTORICAL SPANIEL

A spaniel by the name of "Rover" was traced by Mrs. Peggy Grayson in her exhaustive work on the Field Spaniel breed, entitled *The History and Management of the Field Spaniel*, as being shown as both an English Water Spaniel and a Field Spaniel. This dog does not, however, contribute to modern Field Spaniel pedigrees.

In the 1880s Mr. W. R. Bryden of Beverley in the UK was a famed breeder of Field Spaniels. The trend in those days was to breed for longer and lower dogs, though such exaggerations eventually undermined the breed's popularity.

REGISTERING OFFSPRING

Until 1931 in the UK, offspring of two varieties of spaniels mated together could be registered and subsequently shown as either variety. After 1931, the interbred spaniel registry came into existence. Thereafter, offspring of the matings of two varieties of spaniels had to be registered as interbred.

spaniels. Those spaniels classified as land spaniels were equally as often called "field spaniels." Though many distinct varieties of land spaniel are recorded in historical documents, these varieties were often interbred. Such is the case in the early development of many breeds known today: one variety was mated to another variety to produce yet a third variety. For many years, it was not unusual to see littermates registered as the breed they most closely resembled.

Field Spaniels in the early 1900s were very different in appearance from the Field Spaniels seen today. Following its initial development, the Field Spaniel as a breed met with near-disastrous development. It evolved into a dog so long and so low as to be virtually useless in performing the tasks of a gundog. While the dog show may have contributed to the initial conceptualization and development of the breed, the dog show is theorized to have also contributed to the decline of the Field Spaniel. Dog shows were a relatively new phenomenon and a hobby for the leisure class in those days. However, the term "show dog" was applied somewhat differently in that era in that breeding dogs to show but not to hunt was truly unthinkable.

Dog-show judges then, as now, were only able to judge what was brought before them by exhibitors, and the fad in breeding the Field Spaniel had drifted toward excessive body length and short legs. Reports exist that seem somewhat ludicrous from today's vantage point; these describe judges literally comparing Field

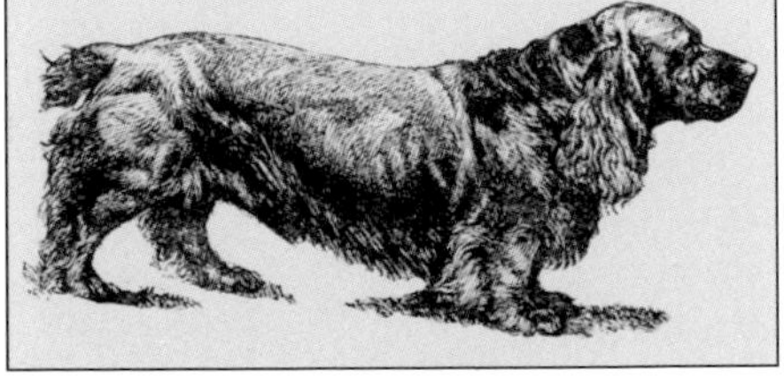

Barum King was supreme in the 1880s, an excellent example of the exaggerations of the period.

Eng. Ch. Wribbenhall Whitewash was an outstanding bitch of yesteryear. Initially solid blacks were the rage, then black and white or red and white with flecking came into favor.

Spaniels side-by-side in an apparent effort to determine which exhibit was the longest in body and lowest on leg. This aberrant development of type removed the Field Spaniel far from the original visions of the breed's early developers. The term "caterpillar dogs" was scathingly used in reference to the breed. The general public who wanted a hunting dog was not impressed and turned away; the Field Spaniel lost his original popularity and has never again regained it.

The extreme version of the breed, which contributed heavily to the near-extinction of the Field Spaniel as a distinct spaniel variety, had an excessively long body with crooked short legs, a beautiful yet heavy head and excessive feathering. These physical traits were the result of outcrosses, most notably to the Sussex Spaniel. Indeed, some early Field Spaniels had more Sussex Spaniel blood than Field, with some individuals owing three-quarters of their bloodline to Sussex and half-Sussex parents.

It is perhaps unfair to credit all of the "long and low" Field Spaniels of that era solely to outcrosses to the Sussex Spaniel. Some evidence also points toward the introduction of the Basset Hound in approximately 1880. Written about by prominent dog writers of the day as a foregone conclusion, this outcross is purported to have added an array of coat colors never previously seen, with large numbers of Field Spaniels produced that were termed "colored." Today's fanciers

CANIS LUPUS

"Grandma, what big teeth you have!" The gray wolf, a familiar figure in fairy tales and legends, has had its reputation tarnished and its population pummeled over the centuries. Yet it is the descendants of this much-feared creature to which we open our homes and hearts. Our beloved dog, *Canis domesticus*, derives directly from the gray wolf, a highly social canine that lives in elaborately structured packs. In the wild, the gray wolf can range from 60 to 175 pounds, standing between 25 and 40 inches in height.

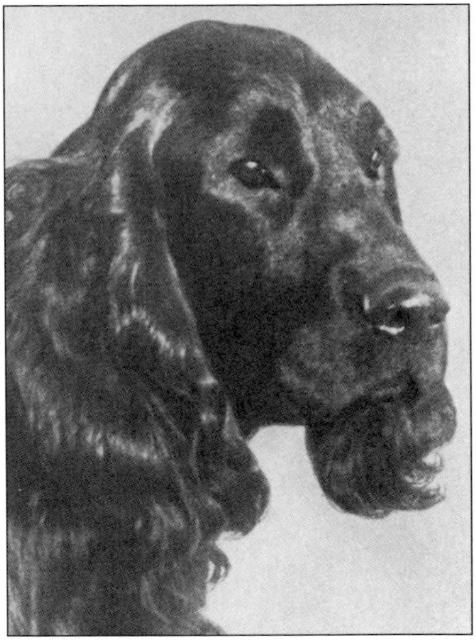

Compare these two heads from dogs of the 1930s. These types, though still appreciated, differ from what is preferred today.

continue this version of history when using the term "Basset front" to describe a rather cabriole-legged appearance not altogether unknown in modern Fields.

While there is one theory that suggests that show-ring wins by the longer and lower type of Field Spaniel contributed to the further development of the "long and low" type of dog, another theory also exists. At the time, sportsmen believed that a spaniel with shorter legs would work heavy cover more effectively than one with relatively longer legs. The logic used was that the shorter-legged dog would be slower of pace and work closer to the hunter, and would thus be easier for the foot hunter to follow. Regardless of the reasons for the development of exaggerated type, whether by virtue of breeding longer and lower dogs in order to win in the conformation ring or to produce a different type of hunting spaniel, the breed went into a decline as a direct result of its extreme appearance.

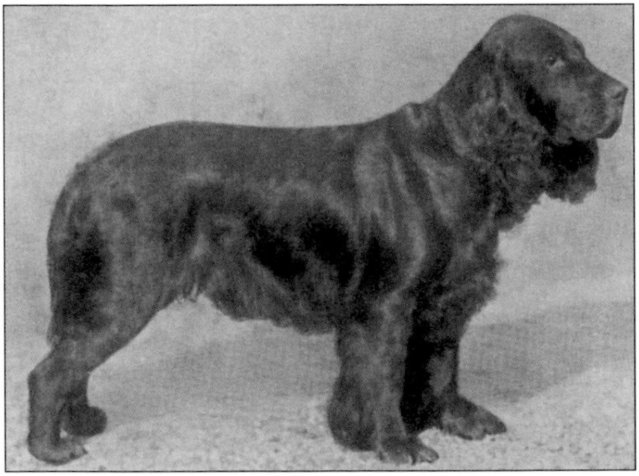

A 1930s favorite was Mr. Owen's Woodbell Perfection, a much-admired Field Spaniel of the day.

Evidence of a further outcross exists, that being to the Irish Water Spaniel. Mrs. Peggy Grayson makes a startling case for this outcross in her tome on the Field Spaniel, citing personal letters from a breeder and fancier of the day who claimed that one of his primary bitches contained Irish Water Spaniel blood. This is hard to dispute, as the breeder is unlikely to have stated that his line contained Irish Water Spaniel genes if it did not. Not content to rely solely on this type of written statement, Mrs. Grayson examined pedigrees and substantially enhanced the argument that the Irish Water Spaniel cross was fact, further theorizing that the beautiful and distinctive head of the Field may well be owed to this very outcross. It is not at all difficult to imagine that this took place when you consider the not-infrequent tendency of Fields to grow curly topknots.

Eng. Ch. Wribbenhall Waiter was a famous champion during the first decade of the 20th century. This lovely dog was owned by Mr. G. Mortimer Smith.

Woodbell Brigand exemplifies the beautiful dogs so desirable in the 1930s. His coat type is similar to that of today's dogs: flat and slightly wavy with some feathering.

Historically, it is undeniably clear and substantiated that the Field Spaniel and the English Cocker Spaniel developed together for many years, up until 1901. Throughout the earliest development of the breed, many fanciers kept both English Cockers and Fields. The liver roan and tan dog Alonzo, who

In the breed's early years, the Fields bred by Mr. G. Mortimer Smith were very popular. His Eng. Ch. Wribbenhall Waterhen is illustrated here.

The Irish Water Spaniel, shown here, is documented as an outcross in certain lines of Field Spaniels, probably contributing its head type (and a few curly topknots) to the breed.

Madame d'Albany was selected to represent the Field Spaniel characteristics in the 1880s.

undeniably contained Sussex Spaniel blood and possibly Irish Water Spaniel and Basset Hound blood as well, is a dominant dog in early pedigrees for both the modern Field Spaniel and English Cocker Spaniel.

The two breeds initially were divided by weight. Solid-colored dogs larger than 25 pounds were recorded as Field Spaniels while those smaller than 25 pounds were recorded as English Cocker Spaniels. Hunters certainly cared little that the larger dogs were Fields while the smaller littermates were Cockers; they were concerned chiefly with the ability of the dogs to hunt.

Luckily, the Field Spaniel was rescued from its initial slide toward extinction by fanciers who had the good sense to reflect upon the original type envisioned by the developers of the breed. While knowledgeable dog writers were claiming the breed to be "dead," certain to dwindle toward extinction, a number of outcrosses to the English Springer Spaniel were made in order to restore a more upstanding type of dog. Sportsmen of the day, who desired a strong spaniel to work thick and formidable cover, persisted in crossing Fields with English Springer Spaniels, with the focus mostly on the working ability of the offspring. The last

In this photo published in 1902, Mr. R. J. Lloyd Price is posing with his Field Spaniel.

The Sussex Spaniel, shown here, was used by Field Spaniel breeders to achieve the lower station, longer body and shorter legs so desirable in the late 1800s and early 1900s.

Many Field Spaniels are excellent water retrievers and respond with enthusiasm to training for hunting over water.

such outcross was recorded in the mid-1950s. This, of course, introduced obvious coloration traits such that the breed standard at one point was deliberately changed to preclude black and white or liver and white exhibits from winning. This was in an effort to distinguish between the English Springer Spaniel and the Field Spaniel. The breed once again evolved, becoming both larger in body and longer in leg while still retaining the substance, movement and characteristic head of the Field Spaniel. Perhaps this was, after all, as the original developers of the 1860s had envisioned.

Despite a small revival, as World War II approached the breed was once again in trouble. Managing to maintain a tenacious toehold on survival, the Field Spaniel progressed precariously during the 1940s in England. Small rays of light were seen as registrations with England's Kennel Club climbed here and there, only to fall again. This pattern continued throughout much of the 1950s and into the mid-1960s when the breed's faint but steady light, which would not be extinguished, began to slowly glow as the Field Spaniel rose from the ashes yet again.

All modern Field Spaniels descend directly from two dogs and two bitches through two important litters of the late 1960s. These Field Spaniels were Ronayne Regal and Gormac Teal, male littermates of the black coat color whelped in 1962; Columbina of Teffont, a black bitch whelped in 1957; and Elmbury Morwenna of Rhiwlas, a

PURE-BRED PURPOSE

Given the vast range of the world's 400 or so pure breeds of dog, it's fair to say that domestic dogs are the most versatile animal in the kingdom. From the tiny 1-pound lap dog to the 200-pound guard dog, dogs have adapted to every need and whim of their human masters. Humans have selectively bred dogs to alter physical attributes like size, color, leg length, mass and skull diameter in order to suit their own needs and fancies. Dogs serve humans not only as companions and guardians but also as hunters, exterminators, shepherds, rescuers, messengers, warriors, babysitters and more!

liver-colored bitch whelped in 1963. In extending the pedigree of any modern Field Spaniel, these four dogs will be found: a remarkably narrow genetic base.

Ronayne Regal figures prominently in modern Field pedigrees through his son, the liver-colored Ridware Emperor, and daughter, the black-colored Eng. Sh. Ch. Mittina Ridware Samantha, both out of Columbina of Teffont. Regal's littermate, Gormac Teal, figures prominently as he sired perhaps the two most famous litters in the modern history of the Field Spaniel. These were the "J" litter from Mittina, out of Eng. Sh. Ch. Mittina Ridware Samantha, and the "A" litter produced under the Elmbury affix out of Juno of Elmbury. You will find "J" and "A" ancestors behind all present-day Field Spaniels. Immediately obvious, then, is the very narrow genetic base of the modern Field, a point to be fully appreciated in contemplation of any breeding of Field Spaniels.

Although the Field Spaniel was first registered by the American Kennel Club in 1894, the breed has never been extremely popular in the United States and continues to be considered a "rare spaniel breed." All of the development

Am./Can. Ch. Soberhill Waterarcher By Mishules, known as "Archie," is a liver import from the UK to the US.

Ch. Marshfield's Daniel Boone was the number-one Field Spaniel all-systems in 2003. He is handled here by Nanette Johnson en route to a Group placement.

that resulted in the modern Field Spaniel occurred in the English homeland of the breed. However, through the efforts of Richard H. Squier (Squier's Kennel) and P. Carl Tuttle (Gunhill Kennel), the Field Spaniel was re-established in the United States in the late 1960s. Slowly but surely, other fanciers noticed the Field Spaniel and, by 1978, there was a sufficient number of fanciers in the US to establish the Field Spaniel Society of America, Inc. Nearly 30 years later, this club remains true to its original purpose: "to encourage and promote quality in the breeding of pure-bred Field Spaniels and to do all possible to bring their natural qualities to perfection." Composed of fanciers located throughout the United States, the Field Spaniel Society of America, Inc. promotes careful stewardship of the breed and is deeply committed to preserving the natural working ability of the breed along with its natural beauty. Today's fanciers are committed to never again allowing the Field Spaniel to diminish to the point where extinction is possible.

In present times, the Field Spaniel has a firm paw in homes throughout the United States though the breed continues to be considered rare. Excelling in many activities, the Field Spaniel, with his personable companionability and loving nature, has won many hearts. Recent years have

Trooper shines in the show ring and in the field. This breed champion shows off his instinctive skills at a working-dog test.

shown Field Spaniels to excel in virtually every event offered by the American Kennel Club for which the breed is eligible. They have won prestigious titles in competitive events such as obedience trials, tracking tests, hunting tests and more, as well as enjoying success in the show ring.

The first Field Spaniel to win the coveted Best in Show award in the US was Ch. Theralan Thrills N Chills. Though such a prestigious win is not often seen, further Field Spaniels also have attained this ultimate prize, most notably Ch. Marshfield's Boy's Night Out, who in recent years has won 11 Best in Show awards and was also the first Field Spaniel to earn a placement in the Sporting Group at the nationally televised annual Westminster Kennel Club show. In the performance arenas, many lofty titles and impressive achievements have been accomplished by Field Spaniels in the different types of competition, which only serves to emphasize the far-reaching abilities of the Field Spaniel as a breed.

The Field Spaniel has a charming and devoted nature along with an endearing expression that can melt any heart.

The Field Spaniel is highly intelligent and loyal, excelling as a home companion, hunting dog and competition dog.

CHARACTERISTICS OF THE

FIELD SPANIEL

"Fields are fun!" is a saying proclaimed on T-shirts worn by numerous American breed aficionados. Worldwide, this statement seems to draw unanimous agreement. Stories of Field Spaniels' exploits are legend among those who are fortunate enough to live with the breed. Their highly developed sense of humor is renowned, and Field Spaniels seem generally to love having the last laugh. Typically good-natured, loyal to family and highly intelligent, the Field Spaniel thrives when included in virtually all everyday activities; indeed, he *expects* that his family will include him!

Fields can be intensely involved in the daily lives of their human packs. This is not a "go lie down and leave me alone" kind of breed. Fields actively seek human companionship and generally will work hard to get it. The breed must have significant daily human interaction to be at its best.

At the same time, the breed is also known for a natural reserve in temperament. Somewhat aloof in initial meetings with strangers, Field Spaniels are at the same time not indifferent. It is as if they simply prefer to look the situation over and reach their own conclusions as to whether or not an individual is worthy of friendship. That Field Spaniels have a perceptive sense in assessing people is a belief strongly affirmed by those who own them. A cool demeanor in initial intro-

If one Field Spaniel is fun, imagine the pleasure of owning, training and showing five dogs at the same time...not to mention the time and commitment!

ductions is strikingly different from a shy temperament that should never be tolerated in the breed.

Both males and females exhibit similar personality traits. Many fanciers, however, do remark on a predisposition of the males to be a bit more willing to snuggle. Females, while also sweet, may be a bit more independent in nature.

Field Spaniels get along with children and other household animals provided they are exposed to them in positive ways starting in young puppyhood. Fields are not typically dog-aggressive, though there are individuals who have shown this tendency. Early socialization plays a large role in avoiding this behavior. When aggression is present, behavior modification techniques should be used. Intervention must rely on methods that avoid overly corrective measures, as these may be seen as aggressive by the dog and thus increase the likelihood of his responding aggressively. In this type of scenario, the aggression escalates.

The Field is a clever and industrious breed. Enclosures must be safe and sturdy to truly contain this curious and agile dog.

Visiting Fields at a breeder's kennel is an exciting and enlightening way to get to know this remarkable breed.

Regarding children and all types of socialization, the Field Spaniel's memory is long, and negative associations may be difficult to overcome without concerted effort. Thus it is necessary that interactions between a puppy and children be supervised. Common sense must prevail when introducing an impressionable puppy to your household.

"Determined" is another word often used in describing the Field

Spaniel. This very tenacity is what makes the breed so very suitable for hunting and many other performance pursuits. This is a different trait than stubbornness or hard-headedness, and behavioral training does not require heavy-handed tactics. The Field's determination means that he will persevere to reach a goal, such as a bird that is difficult to rout and is hunkered down in thick cover.

Fields will also seek to perpetuate gratifying activities such as a good game of retrieve in the back yard. A Field Spaniel may not be content to quit a good game as quickly as his owner, often wandering from person to person with a tennis ball or stick in search of beginning the game anew. This natural penchant for play may be captialized on in training the dog; keep training fun and the Field Spaniel is likely to respond as if saying, "Whatever the game, I'll play."

The drinking and eating behavior of the breed is the source of much comedy, provided the owner has a healthy sense of humor. Fields drinking water are prone to "sharing," such that a partial mouthful of water is often trailed to and from the water dish. Further, mealtimes are eagerly anticipated events for the Field, as it is rare to find one who is a finicky eater. The Field enjoys his food with gusto. Using food rewards is a natural way to proceed in training many behaviors when acclimating the dog to the family's lifestyle. So dedicated are they to eating that Field Spaniels will beg at the dinner table and become food thieves if this behavior is tolerated. Stories abound of disappearing dinner roasts and very happily satiated Field Spaniels.

This penchant for "thievery" may be extended to any items routinely handled or favored by owners. This is not, as it might seem, a case of simple destructiveness. On the contrary, it is generally a Field Spaniel's tribute to how highly the dog thinks of

"Trick or treat!" Ch. Calico's Magnum Force, known to his friends as "Harry," is a show dog, an obedience dog and an agility dog, but his favorite role is as a family dog, always joining in the fun.

DELTA SOCIETY

The human-animal bond propels the work of the Delta Society, striving to improve the lives of people and animals. The Pet Partners Program proves that the lives of people and dogs are inextricably linked. The Pet Partners Program, a national registry, trains and screens volunteers for pet therapy in hospices, nursing homes, schools and rehabilitation centers. Dog-and-handler teams of Pet Partners volunteer in all 50 states, with nearly 7,000 teams making visits annually. About 900,000 patients, residents and students receive assistance each year. If you and your dog are interested in becoming Pet Partners, contact the Delta Society online at www.deltasociety.org.

his human pack. Items frequently used by people pick up the smells of these well-loved humans, becoming prizes in the mind of the Field Spaniel. Library books, remote-control devices and clothing that has been worn and not yet washed are items that the Field Spaniel will find intriguing to pick up, play with and carry.

The breed does shed and this results in fluff-balls of hair that settle overnight. Moderate shedding occurs year-round while heavier shedding is predictable during warmer months. Regular brushing is required to remove dead hair and reduce the amount of sweeping necessary in your household. Furthermore, the Field Spaniel is not averse to mud and other outdoor elements, which will be tracked enthusiastically back into the household. The Field Spaniel is not a breed for a person with "house beautiful" aspirations. However, the breed's natural desire for training and pleasing its owner means that a Field Spaniel can be gently and kindly taught proper home manners. Learning to wait at the door to have his paws wiped before coming indoors and having his face wiped after eating (before he wipes it on the sofa) are routines that are relatively easy to establish.

The vocal range of the breed is the stuff of legend. Field Spaniels are capable of and readily use a wide variety of vocal expressions, ranging from deep-throated barks to high-pitched squeals and distinctive yodels, yips and howls. This is how the Field communicates his pleasure or displeasure, often interacting with his owners in a manner that is nearly human in his ability to express his emotions.

A Field may bark to alert his owner to a suspicious noise while a happy yip may signify enthusiasm for an activity such as being released from his crate, training or work. Fields also are vocally responsive to owners who elicit barking as part of play and other interactions. Fields must be taught when it is appropriate to use their expressive voices; teaching a "Quiet" command is highly recommended. In addition, many Field Spaniels snore during slumber. This can, of course, be mildly annoying when the Field sleeps in your bedroom.

The very intelligence of the breed can and does contribute to behaviors that develop quickly and can be difficult to extinguish, particularly if the dog has been gratified in some way for the behavior. For example, if a puppy's jumping up on his owner in greeting always results in hugs, petting and happy praise, the puppy will not realize that his jumping up might present a problem on a day that his owner is dressed up in fine clothes.

Speaking of the breed's intelligence, Field Spaniels are notorious for discovering how to work their environment to their advantage. Fields investigating the home bathroom have been known to discover how to lift the lid of a toilet seat for a drink of water or even turn on faucets! Field Spaniel owners must indeed have a sense of humor and see things as the dog sees them, since, after all, the good-natured Field Spaniel truly thinks life is to be enjoyed to the fullest.

HEART-HEALTHY

In this modern age of ever-improving cardio-care, no doctor or scientist can dispute the advantages of owning a dog to lower a person's risk of heart disease. Studies have proven that petting a dog, walking a dog and grooming a dog all show positive results toward lowering your blood pressure. The simple routine of exercising your dog—going outside with the dog and walking, jogging or playing catch—is heart-healthy in and of itself. If you are normally less active than your physician thinks you should be, adopting a dog may be a smart option to improve your own quality of life as well as that of another creature.

BREED STANDARD FOR THE
FIELD SPANIEL

INTRODUCTION TO THE BREED STANDARD

Fanciers share the common goal of producing a Field Spaniel of correct type, beautiful enough to win in the show ring yet imbued with innate ability and trainability to work in the field. Indeed, the ideal Field Spaniel is a versatile companion, well suited to many activities. It is important to remember the precarious and colorful history of the Field Spaniel breed. All of the different varieties that created the breed in the beginning, and the necessity for outcrosses to the English Springer Spaniel to avoid extinction, will account for variation in type seen today as these genes line up. It is not unknown, for example, to see Field Spaniels who have a hint, and sometimes more, of Sussex or English Springer Spaniel appearance to the head and body. On occasion, a "houndy" head will arise and, more often, a shorter hound-type coat will appear. Knowledge of the breed standard is mandatory for those who would endeavor to breed and show the Field Spaniel.

While the name "Field Spaniel" is one that somewhat lacks in distinction and often causes confusion, the breed is anything but nondescript. The term "moderate" is one used in the standard of the breed and similarly often causes confusion, as the perception of what is moderate and what is not has a great deal of variation. When looking at the Field Spaniel, one is immediately drawn to the beauty of the head. Even so, the

MEETING THE IDEAL

The American Kennel Club defines a standard as: "A description of the ideal dog of each recognized breed, to serve as an ideal against which dogs are judged at shows." This "blueprint" is drawn up by the breed's recognized parent club, approved by a majority of its membership and then submitted to the AKC for approval.

The AKC states that "An understanding of any breed must begin with its standard. This applies to all dogs, not just those intended for showing." The picture that the standard draws of the dog's type, gait, temperament and structure is the guiding image used by breeders as they plan their programs.

Field Spaniel should not be described as a "head breed" whose virtues are solely resting on the construction of the head, since the overall proportion, balance, depth and bone of the body contribute equally as much to the distinctive appearance of the breed. To emphasize one attribute at the expense of another does the breed no service.

There are a number of official Field Spaniel breed standards recognized by the major kennel clubs around the world. The author here paints a portrait of the breed that reflects the content of all of these standards, a true international rendering of this beautiful breed.

A PORTRAIT OF THE IDEAL FIELD SPANIEL

In considering the proper Field Spaniel head, one is first drawn to the overall impression of nobility and character that are part and parcel of the breed. The Field Spaniel head is very different from that of other spaniel breeds, and there should never be a doubt in the eye of the beholder that one is looking at a Field Spaniel. Even those not well acquainted with the breed will say things such as "I knew this wasn't an 'xyz'," where "xyz" stands for the name of a breed with which they are familiar.

Framed by low-set, long ears with a good amount of silky

Adult Field Spaniel of correct size, substance and proportion.

An American-bred Field Spaniel in magnificent condition, showing off his refined appearance.

feathering, the brown eyes of various shades that suit the coat color are lively yet gentle. The brows should be distinctly apparent and expressive above somewhat widely spaced eyes that are neither loose nor round or protruding. The skull should give the overall impression of length and rectangular appearance when viewed from the side or the top, beginning at the occiput to the tip of the nose. The length of muzzle is never shorter than the length of the backskull and the nasal bone is straight. The lips must fit the muzzle well, without any hint of being pendulous, so that the view of the muzzle from the side is one of soft and gradual curves.

Beneath and above the eyes, the face is aristocratically chiseled, with cheekbones that are relatively flat. The brow is not heavy and has no tendency to overshadow the eyes. The nose color must be solid and tone with the coat color of the dog—brown for liver animals (the darker, the better) and black for Fields of the black coat color. In addition, the nose should be very large with wide-open nostrils and set onto the end of the muzzle without any upward or downward turning; this is, after all, a breed that uses its nose in finding game, and the large nose and straight set-on enhance scenting ability.

The entire head sets onto a neck of good length. A slight arch to the neck from behind the occiput adds to the aristocratic, finely bred appearance when the animal is viewed from the side. The length of the neck should be sufficient so that, when trailing game, the dog does not appear to droop at the shoulder, and objects to be retrieved can be easily picked up off the ground. From the front, the skin of the neck should be well fitted, with just enough laxity that it is able to roll, rather than tear, when the animal is working the dense cover for which he was bred.

The front legs are set well beneath the body of the Field Spaniel, and the prosternum (the foremost portion of the chest) is readily noted so that there is no hint of flatness in the chest. The length of the shoulder blade and upper arm should be nearly identical; short upper arms create undesirable short-strided front movement, which is easily out powered by the strong drive of the rear legs, thereby creating an incorrect sidewinding-type movement. The stride must begin in the shoulder as the legs are driven forward, and imbalance between the length of the shoulder bone and the upper arm will create an inefficient gait. There must be good space between the front legs, never less than a hand-span on an adult dog, yet, at the same time, not so wide as to give any hint of protruding elbows when viewed from the front. Ideal front movement when viewed from the side shows excellent forward reach of the front legs with no hint of choppiness or high-stepping hackneyed movement.

COMPARISON OF PROPORTIONS OF DIFFERENT SPANIELS

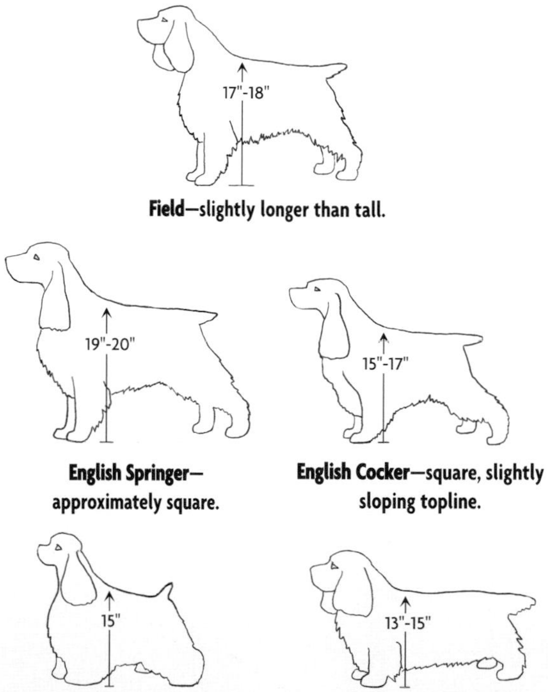

Field—slightly longer than tall.

English Springer—approximately square.

English Cocker—square, slightly sloping topline.

American Cocker—smallest sporting spaniel, square, sloping topline, highest tailset.

Sussex—lowest and heavy boned.

The overall impression of the Field Spaniel body when viewed from the side should at once be that of a good size, though this is not a massive spaniel. There should be just a hint (and no more) of length, and a good depth to the body that begins at the chest and continues through the

MALE VS. FEMALE

Mature male Fields will typically be larger than females in both height and weight, although still within the stated standard for the breed. In other words, if the stated weight range for the standard is 40 to 50 pounds, then the males are more likely to be closer to 50 pounds and the females more likely to be closer to 40 pounds.

Illustration of correct Field Spaniel head.

loin. From the top of the back to the chest should be approximate to the distance from the bottom of the chest to the ground. An overly deep chest, such that the dog appears to have rather less length of leg, or a chest that is shallow, such that the dog appears to have great length of leg, is not correct. Balance here is the key.

The impression of bone should be that it is neither too little nor too much for the overall body. This is a large spaniel in terms of overall body substance without height, and the legs must have sufficient size to support the body.

The topline must be level and firm during movement or when standing still. Dips in the center of the back, such that the back appears sagging like that of an old work horse, and roaching, such that the back appears like that of a racing hound, must be avoided at all costs, as these will lead to a dog who tires more easily during activity. The framework of bone that lies beneath and supports the topline is important to assess. It is the overall length of rib that contributes to the very slightly longer profile of the breed. Fields with short rib cages will often have an immediately noticeable sharp upward curve of loin, or "tuck-up," that rises to create a distinct waist. In these cases, the width of the loin is often too long. The loin must be only gently perceptible.

The set-on of the tail is ideally a natural extension of the line of the back, without any sloping to the croup, as the tail is, after all, an extension of the bony framework of the spine itself. There is no concave dimple where the tail leaves the body as this indicates a tail that is set on too low. At the same time, the tail should not be set overly high so that it is carried well above the line of the back. The tail of the Field Spaniel is customarily docked within a few days of birth, though the standards of some countries allow for natural tails and there are a number of countries that prohibit

COMPARISON OF FIELD SPANIELS IN PROFILE

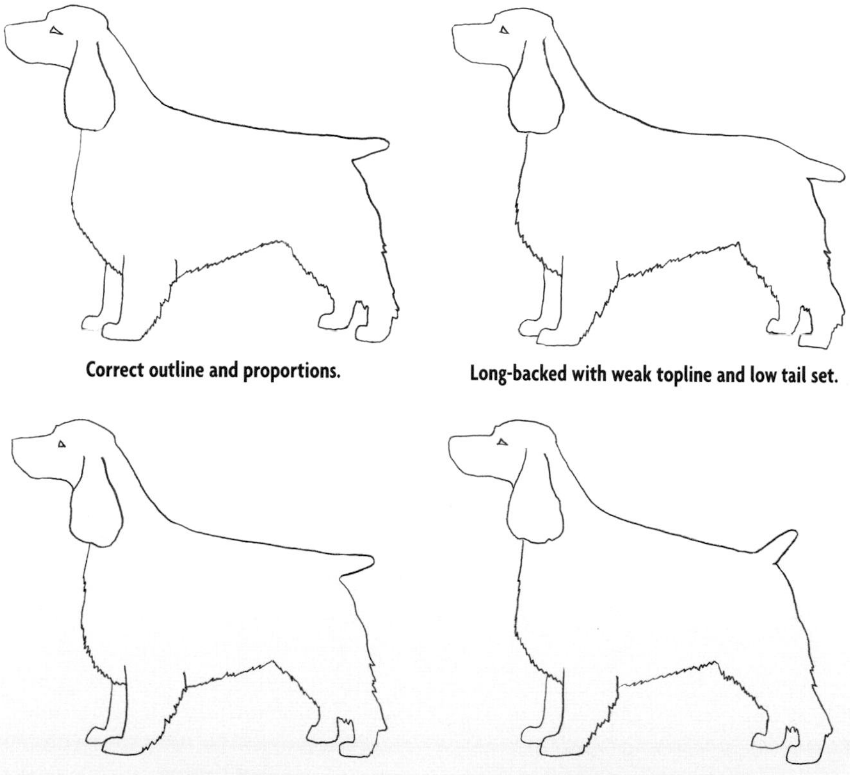

Correct outline and proportions.

Long-backed with weak topline and low tail set.

Back too short.

Exaggerated sloping topline and high tail set like an American Cocker Spaniel.

any docking. When docked, care must be taken to avoid a dock that is overly short. In general, one-third of the overall tail length is retained. In the case of tails, it is better to err on the side of leaving too much rather than too little.

The rear legs should immediately convey the impression of great strength and a well-developed thigh. Angles of the upper and lower leg are moderate such that the entire assembly of the rear leg does not require great backward extension to level the topline as, for example, when the dog is posed for the show ring. Beneath the hock joint, the rear pasterns are short and provide for a powerful characteristic stride that appears effortless while propelling the dog forward. When viewing

BETTER THAN THE AVERAGE DOG

Even though you may never show your dog, you should still read the breed standard. The breed standard tells you more than just physical specifications such as how tall your dog should be; it also describes how he should act, how he should move and what unique qualities make him the breed that he is. You are not investing money in a pure-bred dog so that you can own a dog that "sort of looks like" the breed you're purchasing. You want a typical, handsome representative of the breed, one that all of your friends and family and people you meet out in public will recognize as the breed you've so carefully selected and researched. If the parents of your prospective puppy bear little or no resemblance to the dog described in the breed standard, you should keep searching!

the dog moving in a trotting gait from the side, one should be thoroughly convinced that the dog could maintain the pace all day.

The feet of the Field Spaniel are what endear him to many fanciers. While puppies of many breeds appear to have feet that are large and need to be "grown into," the Field Spaniel carries this appearance for a lifetime. Large feet, with thick pads and well-arched toes that do not spread apart or become flattened in appearance when the dog stands or moves, are ideally made for the most daunting cover when working—or playing—outdoors. These large webbed feet are also ideal for propelling the Field Spaniel through water. Though most Fields are born with dewclaws on the front legs, a few are known to have dewclaws on the rear legs as well. Dewclaws are generally removed within a few days of birth, as they are prone to snagging later in life, which may result in painful injury.

The Field Spaniel is clothed in a thick coat of silky texture with feathering on the ears, on the backs of the front and rear legs and beneath the belly. The coat comes in a variety of colors, though this is not without controversy! Considered a solid-colored dog in that the base coat color covers the entire dog, the most commonly seen colors are liver and black. The liver coat is manifested in a variety of shades from that of a milk chocolate to a dark bittersweet-chocolate color. Hints of gold in a light liver color coat are thought by many to be a throwback to the great amount of Sussex Spaniel blood introduced into the breed in the early part of the 20th century.

Patches of white may appear on the chests of liver or black Field Spaniels, though nowhere else without penalty in the show ring. While many fanciers like the look of the Field Spaniel with a narrow "necktie" of white, less white is typically viewed more favorably. Any white that extends from shoulder to shoulder in width, as in a "shirt front," is definitely too much. Tan points may be seen on any coat color (including roan), appearing on the eyebrows, sides of the muzzle (sometimes extending back to the cheeks), chest, front pasterns and rear pasterns as well as a typical patch beneath the tail. Ideally, the tan is a rich golden color and not washed out in appearance, and there may be dark "pencil" marks on the feet that only serve to enhance the tan coloring.

The roan coloration is perhaps where the most controversy exists in terms of how the term "roan" is defined. There is much disagreement among fanciers as to the proper definition of the term. Strictly defined by some fanciers as an intermingling of colored and white hairs such that the dog may take on a "silvered" appearance while having some patches of dark coat color, other fanciers expand the definition to include tiny ticking spots in a base white coat color. Dogs colored in this manner, which may appear to be black and white or liver and white until you ruffle the coat to determine that there is intermingling of the colored and white

The two main coat colors in the Field Spaniel are black and liver. Although a solid-colored dog, some white on the chest is acceptable as long it is not too wide of a patch.

Head study of a champion, Am./Can. Ch. Soberhill Waterarcher By Mishules.

hairs, are also defined as "roan" by some breeders. There is, at this point, a fairly even split among those using either definition so that the somewhat muddy explanation of the term "roan" is likely to be present for some time to come. Coat color is the least important attribute among the abilities of a Field Spaniel as a companion in your home or as a hunter extraordinaire, though it sometimes has a bearing on how well a dog does in the show ring.

FIELD SPANIEL

SELECTING A FIELD PUPPY

In choosing a Field Spaniel puppy, first and foremost consider your aspirations in acquiring a Field Spaniel. Do you wish to show your dog in the conformation ring? Do you want a superb bird dog? Do you want a household companion? Or, do you—as do many who choose the Field Spaniel—want a dog that can do all of these? While faults, such as too much white on the chest or a head style that varies too far from the standard, may effectively rule a puppy out as a show prospect, faults of this nature are not going to make a difference for a Field Spaniel whose primary occupation will be as a hunting partner or household companion. Most Field Spaniel litters have an amount of variation within the litter in terms of type, personality and even size; it is rare that all puppies in any single litter would be show prospects or that all puppies would show the interest in birds desirable in a hunting companion. Know what your goals are before you begin contacting breeders; this will be helpful to the breeder in determining if there is an appropriate puppy for you in any particular litter. With average litter size of six or seven

The Field Spaniel's expression is irresistible at any age.

A SHOW PUPPY

If you plan to show your puppy, you must first deal with a reputable breeder who shows his dogs and has had some success in the conformation ring. The puppy's pedigree should include one or more champions in the first and second generation. You should be familiar with the breed and breed standard so you can know what qualities to look for in your puppy. The breeder's observations and recommendations also are invaluable aids in selecting your future champion. If you consider an older puppy, be sure that the puppy has been properly socialized with people and not isolated in a kennel without substantial daily human contact.

SIGNS OF A HEALTHY PUPPY

Healthy puppies are robust little fellows who are alert and active, sporting shiny coats and supple skin. They should not appear lethargic, bloated or pot-bellied, nor should they have flaky skin or runny or crusted eyes or noses. Their stools should be firm and well formed, with no evidence of blood or mucus.

puppies, there can be a good selection available.

Once you know what your goals are in acquiring a puppy, the next, more important, aspect to consider is overall health. After all, you will have this Field Spaniel for the next dozen or more years and nothing can break the heart more quickly than a well-loved puppy that is not sound in body or mind. Much to the dismay of concerned Field Spaniel breeders worldwide, even the most cautious breeding of two parents testing normal for all known "testable" problems may produce a puppy who will show problems. Fortunately, health problems known in the Field Spaniel breed are fewer in number in comparison with many other breeds, particularly in consideration of the narrow genetic base of the Field. General good health seems to be a trait with which the breed, overall, is fortunate to be endowed, and Field Spaniel breeders in general are cautious about breeding for the healthiest puppies possible. However, there are concerns that appear often enough to warrant mention. As you look for a Field Spaniel puppy, be sure to directly discuss any health concerns you may have with breeders. Issues to discuss include the following:

Hip dysplasia: Hip dysplasia is an abnormal development of the ball-and-socket apparatus of the hip joint, which is typically progressive with the growth and development from puppy to adult dog. Symptoms have wide variation, from almost none perceptible to extreme pain and lameness. Virtually every country has veterinary testing schemes available to rate the conformation of dogs' hip joints. While it is not a fail-safe preventive, as factors other than heredity come into play, research data worldwide concludes that breeding two parents with normal hip conformation tends to produce a higher percentage of puppies with healthy hips. In the US, breeders should submit hip x-rays to the Orthopedic Foundation for Animals (OFA) for evaluation and only breed dogs that receive OFA clearances; ask your breeder to see the litter's parents' OFA documentation. Field Spaniel breeders take this potential problem seriously and breed carefully to try, as best as possible, to avoid it.

Eye abnormalities: These include entropion (eyelids that turn inward), ectropion (eyelids that are turn somewhat outward to create a loose eye, showing haw) and cataracts. PRA (progressive retinal atrophy) is another condition diagnosed in Field Spaniels that leads to total blindness; luckily, there have been few dogs diagnosed with this particular disorder and today's breeders are careful that this remains a very rare problem. Many eye abnormalities are considered genetically transferred; breeders should have annual CERF (Canine Eye Registration Foundation) exams done on their dogs and have current clearances on all breeding stock.

Hypothyroidism: Low levels of thyroid hormones have been well known in the breed for a number of years. While there is some controversy over the heritable nature of the problem, it is safe to say that breeding two parents who have been tested and have normal thyroid function is likely to produce a higher percentage of puppies with normal thyroid function. Although breeders try to avoid this problem in their lines, hypothyroidism is among the most

Standing pretty at ten weeks old, "Freddie" (who became Ch. Calico's If Looks Could Kill RN) looks ahead to a bright future with titles in the show ring and rally competition.

MAKE A COMMITMENT

Dogs are most assuredly man's best friend, but they are also a lot of work. When you add a puppy to your family, you also are adding to your daily responsibilities for years to come. Dogs need more than just food, water and a place to sleep. They also require training (which can be ongoing throughout the lifetime of the dog), activity to keep them physically and mentally fit and hands-on attention every day, plus grooming and healthcare. Your life as you now know it may well disappear! Are you prepared for such drastic changes?

Do You Know about Hip Dysplasia?

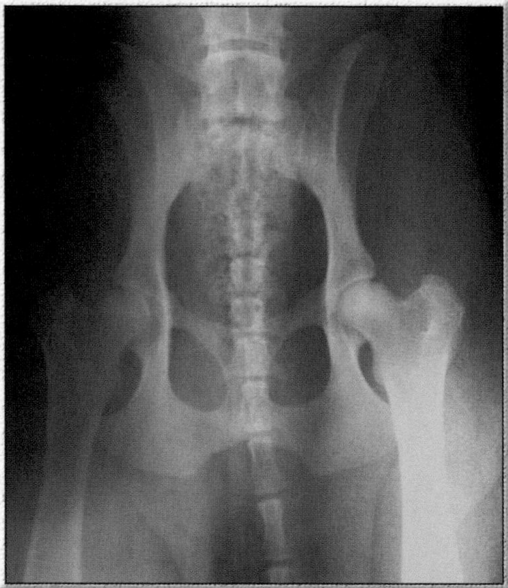

X-ray of a dog with "Good" hips.

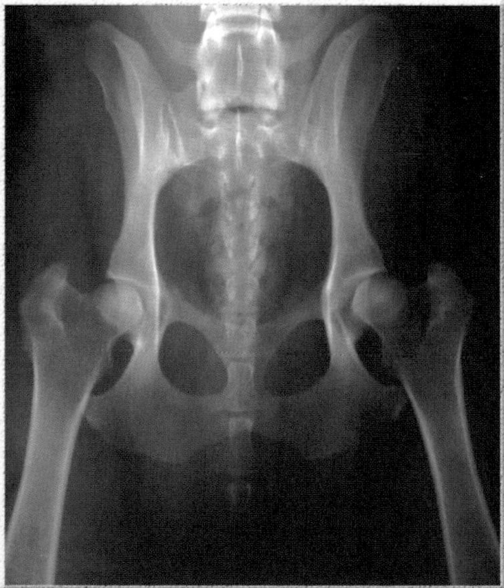

X-ray of a dog with "Moderate" dysplastic hips.

Hip dysplasia is a fairly common condition found in pure-bred dogs. When a dog has hip dysplasia, his hind leg has an incorrectly formed hip joint. By constant use of the hip joint, it becomes more and more loose, wears abnormally and may become arthritic.

Hip dysplasia can only be confirmed with an x-ray, but certain symptoms may indicate a problem. Your dog may have a hip dysplasia problem if he walks in a peculiar manner, hops instead of smoothly runs, uses his hind legs in unison (to keep the pressure off the weak joint), has trouble getting up from a prone position or always sits with both legs together on one side of his body.

As the dog matures, he may adapt well to life with a bad hip, but in a few years the arthritis develops and many dogs with hip dysplasia become crippled.

Hip dysplasia is considered an inherited disease and only can be diagnosed definitively by x-ray when the dog is two years old, although symptoms often appear earlier. Some experts claim that a special diet might help your puppy outgrow the bad hip, but the usual treatments are surgical. The removal of the pectineus muscle, the removal of the round part of the femur, reconstructing the pelvis and replacing the hip with an artificial one are all surgical interventions that are expensive, but they are usually very successful. Follow the advice of your veterinarian.

treatable of all problems, involving annual blood testing and inexpensive daily medication.

You can often get a feel for the general health of a breeder's stock by visiting the kennel if at all possible. Realistically, this is not always something that can be done given the rarity of the breed and the various locations of breeders. For example, show prospects may be imported from one country to another, and in some countries such as the United States, obtaining a Field Spaniel puppy may well mean that the puppy must travel by airplane from one coast to the other! In these cases, you will need to do most of your investigation by telephone.

Start by contacting the Field Spaniel Society of America's breeder referral committee. Once you begin talking with breeders, whether by phone or in person, ask questions about the health, temperament and ages of parents, and then go on to ask about grandparents and great-grandparents. Did these dogs live to older ages or did they die young? What health problems has the breeder encountered? Be wary of any breeder who has bred more than a litter or two and who flatly states that he has never produced a dog with any sort of problem! If you are fortunate enough to be able to visit the breeder, look at and interact with the dogs residing with the breeder and assess their overall appearance of health and vitality.

GETTING ACQUAINTED

When visiting a litter, ask the breeder for suggestions on how best to interact with the puppies. If possible, get right into the middle of the pack and sit down with them. Observe which pups climb into your lap and which ones shy away. Toss a toy for them to chase and bring back to you. It's easy to fall in love with the puppy who picks you, but keep your future objectives in mind before you make your final decision.

Reviewing pedigrees can be helpful in some instances. For example, if your goal is a show dog that you hope will win in the conformation ring, check for several generations of champions in the pedigree. Similarly, if your goal is a hunting companion, look for evidence of proven hunting ability in the pedigree. A breeder should easily be able to

NEW RELEASES

Most breeders release their puppies between eight and ten weeks of age. A breeder who allows puppies to leave the litter at five or six weeks of age may be more concerned with profit than with the puppies' welfare. However, some breeders of show or working lines may hold one or more top-quality puppies longer, occasionally until three or four months of age, in order to evaluate the puppies' careers or show potential and decide which one(s) they will keep for themselves.

provide you with a readable pedigree that spans several generations. Titles should appear in the generations closest to the pup, as titles too far back in the pedigree mean little.

If you are able to visit a litter in person, approach the visitation with your head and not your heart. The reticent puppy may tug at your heart but may not be the best prospect if you have a busy household or you wish to have a dog that virtually shouts "look at me" to a dog-show judge. On the other hand, this same puppy with a reserved but gentle nature may be the ideal companion in other situations.

Look for obvious signs of health: eyes should be clear without tearing; there should be no obvious structural problems such as lameness; there should be no coughing or raspiness to the breathing; and the overall litter should simply have the appearance of health—physically clean and accustomed to being handled by people.

Finally, inasmuch as you are interviewing the breeder, be prepared to have the breeder interview you! Field Spaniel breeders are generally a cautious lot and care deeply about the placement of each individual puppy in the proper home for that puppy. Be prepared for some in-depth questions about your home, lifestyle, overall experience with dogs and so forth. Give honest answers, as this will assist the breeder greatly in determining if there is a puppy in the litter that will suit your home and goals. A good match between the individual puppy and owner is essential to a happy dog-owner relationship.

A COMMITTED NEW OWNER

By now you should understand what makes the Field Spaniel a most unique and special dog, one that may fit nicely into your family and lifestyle. If you have researched breeders, you should be able to recognize a knowledgeable and responsible Field Spaniel breeder who cares not only about his pups but also about what kind of owner you will be. If you have traveled farther on your new journey, you have found a litter, or possibly two, of quality Field Spaniel pups.

A visit with the puppies and their breeder should be an education in itself. Breed research, breeder selection and puppy visitation are very important aspects of finding the puppy of your dreams. Beyond that, these things also lay the foundation for a successful future with your pup. Puppy personalities within each litter vary, from the shy and easygoing puppy to the one who is dominant and assertive, with most pups falling somewhere in between. By spending time with the puppies

The breeder should show you the dam of the litter along with the pups. If the dam is not on the premises, you should continue your puppy search elsewhere.

PEDIGREE VS. REGISTRATION CERTIFICATE

Too often new owners are confused between these two important documents. Your puppy's pedigree, essentially a family tree, is a written record of a dog's genealogy of three generations or more. The pedigree will show you the names as well as performance titles of all dogs in your pup's background. Your breeder must provide you with a registration application, with his part properly filled out. You must complete the application and send it to the AKC with the proper fee. Every puppy must come from a litter that has been AKC-registered by the breeder, born in the US and from a sire and dam that are also registered with the AKC.

The seller must provide you with complete records to identify the puppy. The AKC requires that the seller provide the buyer with the following: breed; sex, color and markings; date of birth; litter number (when available); names and registration numbers of the parents; breeder's name; and date sold or delivered.

In the hands of dedicated breeders, the Field Spaniel is lovingly maintained and bred for consistency and soundness.

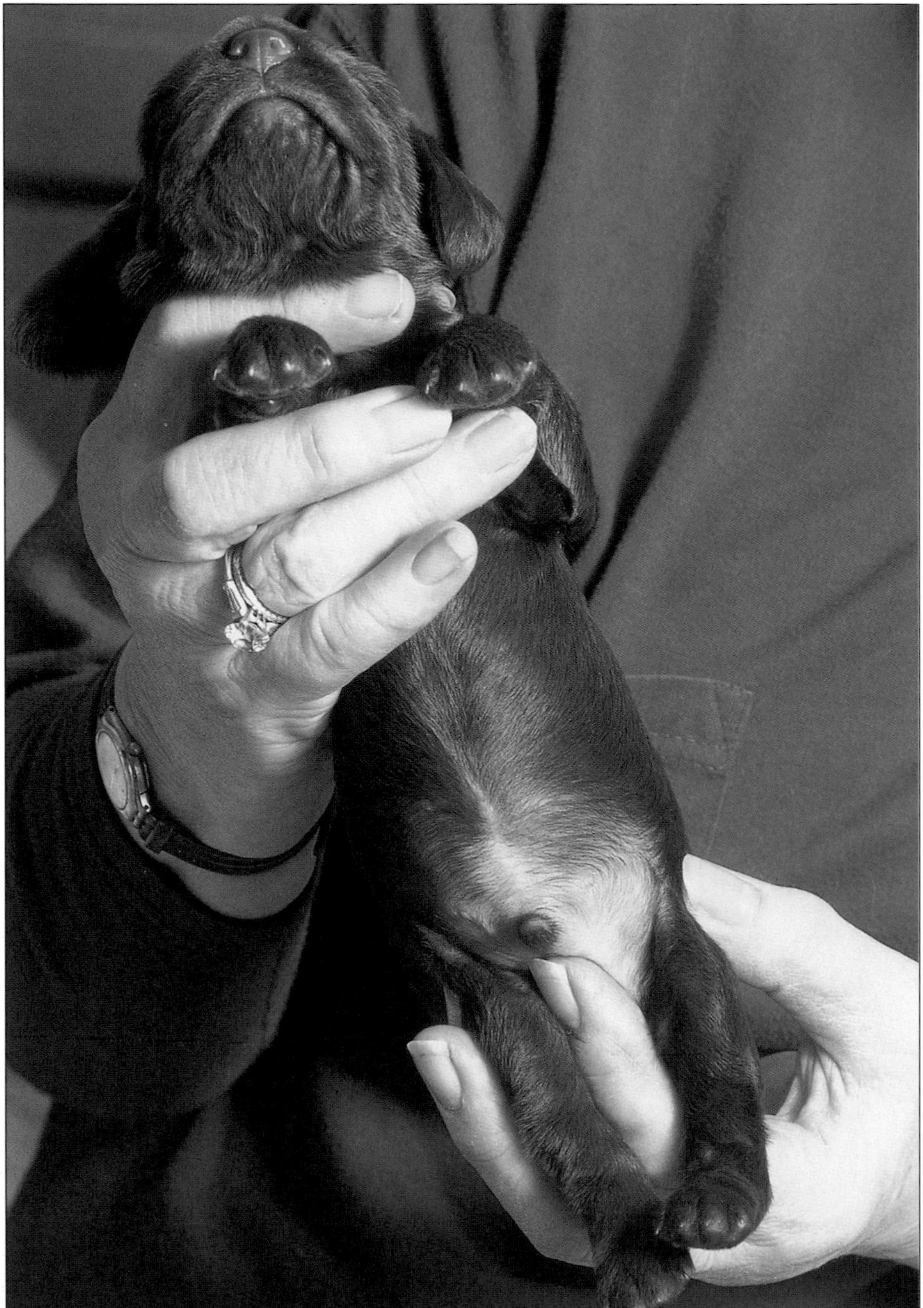

you will be able to recognize certain behaviors and what these behaviors indicate about each pup's temperament. Which type of pup will complement your family dynamics is best determined by observing the puppies in action within their "pack." Your breeder's expertise and recommendations are also valuable. Although you may fall in love with a bold and brassy male, the breeder may suggest that another pup would be best for you. The breeder's experience in rearing Field Spaniel pups and matching their temperaments with appropriate humans offers the best assurance that your pup will meet your needs and expectations. The type of puppy that you select is just as important as your decision that the Field Spaniel is the breed for you.

The decision to live with a Field Spaniel is a serious commitment and not one to be taken lightly. This puppy is a living sentient being that will be dependent on you for basic survival for his entire life. Beyond the basics of survival—food, water, shelter and protection—he needs much, much more. The new pup needs love, nurturing and a proper canine education to mold him into a responsible, well-behaved canine citizen. Your Field Spaniel's health and good manners will need consistent monitoring and regular "tune-ups," so your job as a responsible dog owner will be ongoing throughout every stage of his life. If you are not prepared to accept these responsibilities and commit to them for at least the next 12 years, then you are not prepared to own a dog of any breed.

It is the author's intention to emphasize the commitment of dog ownership, as the Field Spaniel truly requires an active, interactive owner. Certainly, with some time and patience, your new charge will grow up to be your most loyal friend, devoted to you unconditionally.

YOUR FIELD SPANIEL SHOPPING LIST

Just as expectant parents prepare a nursery for their baby, so should you ready your home for the arrival of your Field Spaniel pup. If you have the necessary puppy supplies purchased and in place

CREATE A SCHEDULE

Puppies thrive on sameness and routine. Offer meals at the same time each day, take him out at regular times for potty trips and do the same for play periods and outdoor activity. Make note of when your puppy naps and when he is most lively and energetic, and try to plan his day around those times. Once he is house-trained and more predictable in his habits, he will be better able to tolerate changes in his schedule.

before he comes home, it will ease the puppy's transition from the warmth and familiarity of his mom and littermates to the brand-new environment of his new home and human family. You will be too busy to stock up and prepare your house after your pup comes home, that's for sure! Imagine how a pup must feel upon being transported to a strange new place. It's up to you to comfort him and to let your little pup know that he is going to be happy with you.

CRATE EXPECTATIONS

To make the crate more inviting to your puppy, you can offer his first meal or two inside the crate, always keeping the crate door open so that he does not feel confined. Keep a favorite toy or two in the crate for him to play with while inside. You can also cover the crate at night with a lightweight sheet to make it more den-like and remove the stimuli of household activity. Never put him into his crate as punishment or as you are scolding him, since he will then associate his crate with negative situations and avoid going there.

Food and Water Bowls

Your puppy will need separate bowls for his food and water. Stainless steel bowls are generally preferred over plastic bowls since they sterilize better and pups are less inclined to chew on the metal. Heavy-duty ceramic bowls are popular, but consider how often you will have to pick up those heavy bowls. Buy adult-sized bowls, as your puppy will grow into them before you know it.

The Dog Crate

If you think that crates are tools of punishment and confinement for when a dog has misbehaved, think again. Most breeders and almost all trainers recommend a crate as the preferred house-training aid as well as for all-around puppy training and safety. Because dogs are natural den creatures that prefer cave-like environments, the benefits of crate use are many. The crate provides the puppy with his very own "safe house," a cozy place to sleep, take a break or seek comfort with a favorite toy; a travel aid to house your dog when on the road, at motels or at the vet's office; a training aid to help teach your puppy proper toileting habits; and a place of solitude when non-dog people happen to drop by and don't want a lively puppy—or even a well-behaved adult dog—saying hello or begging for attention.

Crates come in several types, although the wire crate and the fiberglass airline-type crate are the most popular. Both are safe and your puppy will adjust to either one, so the choice is up to you. The wire crates offer better visibility for the pup as well as better ventilation. Many of the wire crates easily fold into suitcase-size carriers. The fiberglass crates, similar to those used by the airlines for animal transport, are sturdier and more den-like. However, the fiberglass crates do not fold down and are less ventilated than wire crates, which can be problematic in hot weather. Some of the newer crates are made of heavy plastic mesh; they are very lightweight and fold up into slim-line suitcases. However, a mesh crate might not be suitable for a pup with manic chewing habits.

Don't bother with a puppy-sized crate. Although your Field Spaniel will be a wee fellow when you bring him home, he will grow up in the blink of an eye and your puppy crate will be useless. Purchase a crate that will accommodate an adult Field Spaniel. A crate measuring between 32 inches (for smaller females) and 36 inches (for larger males) long, and of appropriate height and width to allow the adult to fully stand and turn around, will be suitable.

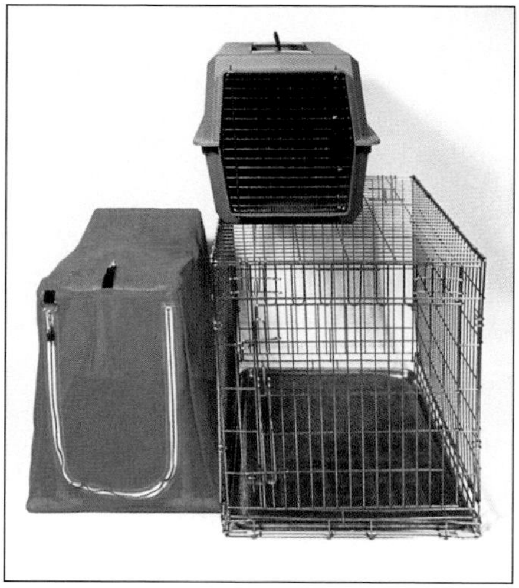

The three most popular crate types: mesh on the left, wire on the right and fiberglass on top.

Bedding and Crate Pads

Your puppy will enjoy some type of soft bedding in his "room" (the crate), something he can snuggle into to feel cozy and secure. Old towels or blankets are good choices for a young pup, since he may (and probably will) have a toileting accident or two in the crate or decide to chew on the bedding material. Once he is fully trained and out of the early chewing stage, you can replace the puppy bedding with a permanent crate pad if you prefer. Crate pads and other dog beds run the gamut from inexpensive to high-end doggie-designer styles, but don't splurge on the good stuff until you are sure that your puppy is reliable and won't tear it up or make a mess on it.

TOYS 'R SAFE

The vast array of tantalizing puppy toys is staggering. Stroll through any pet shop or pet-supply outlet and you will see that the choices can be overwhelming. However, not all dog toys are safe or sensible. Most very young puppies enjoy soft woolly toys that they can snuggle with and carry around. (You know they have outgrown them when they shred them up!) Avoid toys that have buttons, tabs or other enhancements that can be chewed off and swallowed. Soft toys that squeak are fun, but make sure your puppy does not disembowel the toy and remove (and swallow) the squeaker. Toys that rattle or make noise can excite a puppy, but they present the same danger as the squeaky kind and so require supervision. Hard rubber toys that bounce can also entertain a pup, but make sure that the toy is too big for your pup to swallow.

PUPPY TOYS

Just as infants and older children require objects to stimulate their minds and bodies, puppies need toys to entertain their curious brains, wiggly paws and achy teeth. A fun array of safe doggie toys will help satisfy your puppy's chewing instincts and distract him from gnawing on the leg of your antique chair or your new leather sofa. Most puppy toys are cute and look as if they would be a lot of fun, but not all are necessarily safe or good for your puppy, so use caution when you go puppy-toy shopping.

During teething, the need to chew will escalate as expected with that developmental phenomenon. Field Spaniels who are bored are also known to resort to chewing to entertain themselves. It is up to you to provide appropriate chew items for your dog. The best "chewcifiers" are sturdy nylon and hard rubber bones that are safe to gnaw on and come in sizes appropriate for all age groups and breeds. Be especially careful of natural bones, which can splinter or develop dangerous sharp edges; pups can easily swallow or choke on those bone splinters. Veterinarians often tell of surgical nightmares involving bits of splintered bone, because in addition to the danger of choking, the sharp pieces can damage the intestinal tract.

An appropriate and generally inexpensive chew item is a raw

beef shank (leg) bone available from most butchers in lengths of 6 to 8 inches. Rawhide chews, chew hooves and other similar items are not advisable. Rawhide chews quickly become a slimy, sticky mass with an aggressive chewer, whereas chew hooves may break into sharp pieces when chewed. Both are easy to swallow and have been known to result in digestive ailments, sometimes requiring surgical intervention.

Soft woolly toys are special puppy favorites. They come in a wide variety of cute shapes and sizes; some look like little stuffed animals. Puppies love to shake them up and toss them about, or simply carry them around. Be careful of fuzzy toys that have button eyes or noses that your pup could chew off and swallow, and make sure that he does not disembowel a squeaky toy to remove the squeaker! Remove these toys at any sign of their being "de-stuffed" or chewed apart. Braided rope toys are similar in that they are fun to chew and toss around, but they shred easily and the strings are easy to swallow. The strings are not digestible and, if the puppy doesn't pass them in his stool, he could end up at the vet's office. As with rawhides, your puppy should be closely monitored with rope toys.

If you believe that your pup has ingested a piece of one of his toys, check his stools for the next couple of days to see if he passes the item when he defecates. At the same time, also watch for signs of intestinal distress. A call to your veterinarian might be in order to get his advice and be on the safe side.

An all-time favorite toy for puppies (young and old!) is the empty gallon milk jug. Hard plastic

Teething pups appreciate something soft to chomp on.

KEEP OUT OF REACH

Most dogs don't browse around your medicine cabinet, but accidents do happen! The drug acetaminophen, the active ingredient in certain popular over-the-counter pain relievers, can be deadly to dogs and cats if ingested in large quantities. Acetaminophen toxicity, caused by the dog's swallowing 15 to 20 tablets, can be manifested in abdominal pains within a day or two of ingestion, as well as liver damage. If you suspect your dog has swiped a bottle of medication, get the dog to the vet immediately so that the vet can induce vomiting and cleanse the dog's stomach.

juice containers—46 ounces or more—are also excellent. Such containers make lots of noise when they are batted about, and puppies go crazy with delight as they play with them. However, they don't often last very long, so be sure to remove and replace them when they get chewed up.

A word of caution about homemade toys: be careful with your choices of non-traditional play objects. Never use old shoes or socks, since a puppy cannot distinguish between the old ones on which he's allowed to chew and the new ones in your closet that are strictly off limits. That principle applies to anything that resembles something that you don't want your puppy to chew.

Collars

A lightweight nylon collar is the best choice for a very young pup. Quick-click collars are easy to put on and remove, and they can be adjusted as the puppy grows. Introduce him to his collar as soon as he comes home to get him accustomed to wearing it. He'll get used to it quickly and won't mind a bit. Make sure that it is snug enough that it won't slip off, yet loose enough to be comfortable for the pup. You should be able to slip two fingers between the collar and his neck. Check the collar often, as puppies grow in spurts, and his collar can become too tight almost overnight.

Leashes

A 6-foot nylon lead is an excellent choice for a young puppy. It is lightweight and not as tempting to chew as a leather lead. You can switch to a 6-foot leather lead after your pup has grown and is used to walking politely on a lead. For initial puppy walks and house-training purposes, you should invest in a shorter lead so that you have more control over the puppy. At first, you don't want him wandering too far away from you, and when taking him out for toileting you will want to keep him in the specific area chosen for his potty spot.

Once the puppy is heel-trained with a traditional leash, you can consider purchasing a retractable lead. A retractable lead is excellent for walking adult dogs that are already leash-wise. This type of lead expands to allow the dog to roam farther away from you and explore a wider area when out walking, and also retracts when you need to keep him close to you.

HOME SAFETY FOR YOUR PUPPY

The importance of puppy-proofing cannot be overstated. In addition to making your house comfortable for your Field Spaniel's arrival, you also must make sure that your house is safe for your puppy before you bring him home. There are countless hazards in the owner's personal living environment that a

A Dog-Safe Home

The dog-safety police are taking you on a house tour. Let's go room by room and see how safe your own home is for your new pup. The following items are doggy dangers, so either they must be removed or the dog should be monitored or not have access to these areas.

Living Room

- house plants (some varieties are poisonous)
- fireplace or wood-burning stove
- paint on the walls (lead-based paint is toxic)
- lead drapery weights (toxic lead)
- lamps and electrical cords
- carpet cleaners or deodorizers

Outdoor

- swimming pool
- pesticides
- toxic plants
- lawn fertilizers

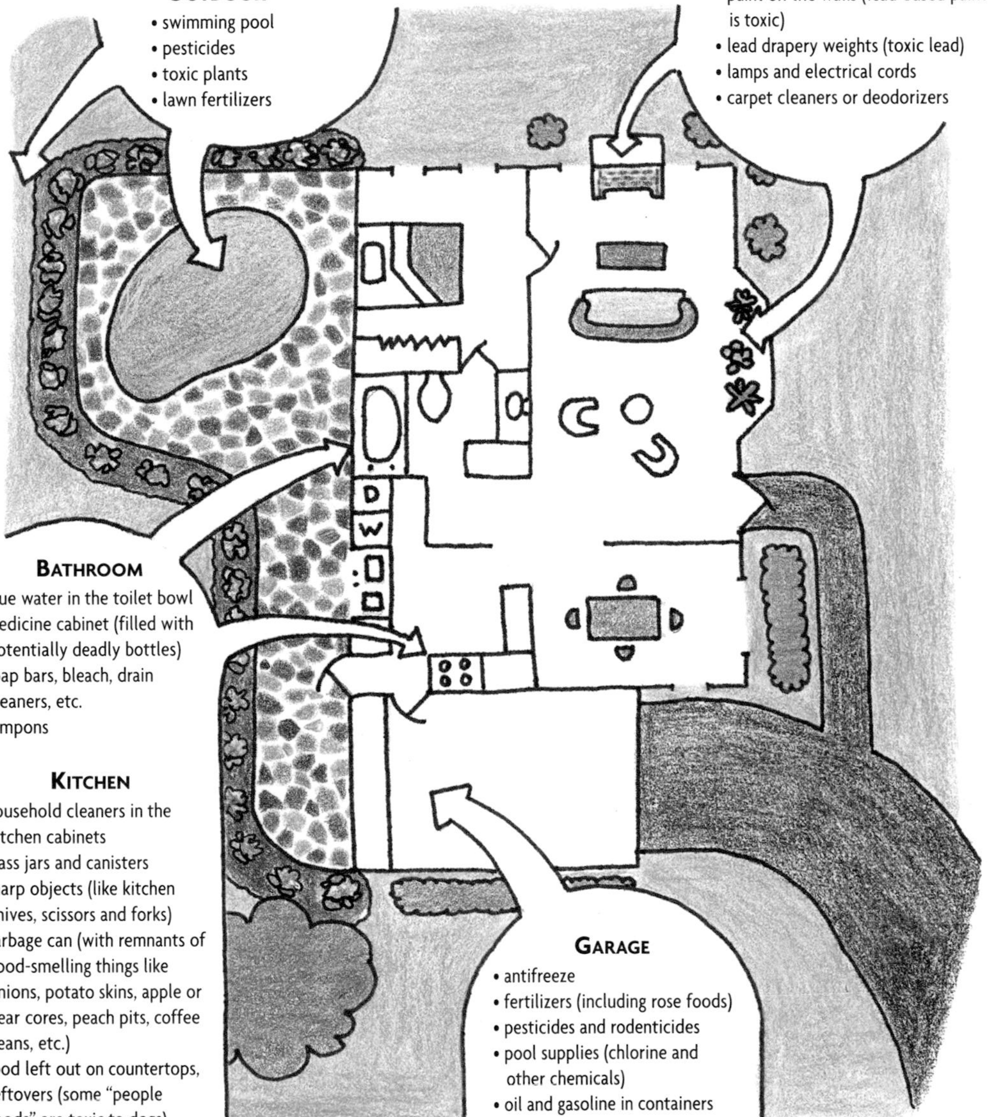

Bathroom

- blue water in the toilet bowl
- medicine cabinet (filled with potentially deadly bottles)
- soap bars, bleach, drain cleaners, etc.
- tampons

Kitchen

- household cleaners in the kitchen cabinets
- glass jars and canisters
- sharp objects (like kitchen knives, scissors and forks)
- garbage can (with remnants of good-smelling things like onions, potato skins, apple or pear cores, peach pits, coffee beans, etc.)
- food left out on countertops, leftovers (some "people foods" are toxic to dogs)

Garage

- antifreeze
- fertilizers (including rose foods)
- pesticides and rodenticides
- pool supplies (chlorine and other chemicals)
- oil and gasoline in containers
- sharp objects, electrical cords and power tools

pup can sniff, chew, swallow or destroy. Many are obvious; others are not. Do a thorough advance house check to remove or rearrange those things that could hurt your puppy, keeping any potentially dangerous items out of areas to which he will have access.

Electrical cords are especially dangerous, since puppies view them as irresistible chew toys. Unplug and remove all exposed cords or fasten them beneath baseboards where the puppy cannot reach them. Veterinarians and firefighters can tell you horror stories about electrical burns and house fires that resulted from puppy-chewed electrical cords. Consider this a most serious precaution for your puppy and the rest of your family.

Scout your home for tiny objects that might be seen at a pup's eye level. Keep medication bottles and cleaning supplies well out of reach, and do the same with waste baskets and other trash containers. It goes without saying that you should not use rodent poison or other toxic chemicals in any puppy area and that you must keep such containers safely locked up. You will be amazed at how many places a curious puppy can discover!

Once your house has cleared inspection, check your yard. A sturdy fence, well embedded into the ground to prevent digging under, will give your dog a safe place to play and potty. Field Spaniels are notorious problem-solvers, and this includes turning their considerable attention to the activity of escaping confinement. While certainly not all Field Spaniels work to escape confinement, there are enough stories of Field Spaniels who climb, dig and/or jump that the pet owner must consider the potential. In general, a 6-foot-tall fence is adequate; however, some persistent Field Spaniels may require an escape-proof top cover on a kennel run. Check the fence or run regu-

TOXIC PLANTS

Plants are natural puppy magnets, but many can be harmful, even fatal, if ingested by a puppy or adult dog. Scout your yard and home interior and remove any plants, bushes or flowers that could be even mildly dangerous. It could save your puppy's life. You can obtain a complete list of toxic plants from your veterinarian, at the public library or by looking online.

larly and make repairs as needed. If there is a weak spot or space to squeeze through, you can be sure that a determined Field Spaniel will discover it.

The garage and shed can be hazardous places for a pup, as things like fertilizers, chemicals and tools are usually kept there. It's best to keep these areas off limits to the pup. Antifreeze is especially dangerous to dogs, as they find the taste appealing and it takes only a few licks from the driveway to kill a dog, puppy or adult, small breed or large.

VISITING THE VETERINARIAN

A good veterinarian is your Field Spaniel puppy's best health-insurance policy. If you do not already have a vet, ask friends and experienced dog people in your area for recommendations so that you can select a vet before you bring your Field Spaniel puppy home. Also arrange for your puppy's first veterinary examination beforehand, since many vets do not have appointments immediately available and your puppy should visit the vet within a day or so of coming home.

It's important to make sure your puppy's first visit to the vet is a pleasant and positive one. The vet should take great care to befriend the pup and handle him gently to make their first meeting a positive experience. The vet will give the pup a thorough physical examination and set up a schedule for vaccinations and other necessary wellness visits. Be sure to show your vet any health and inoculation records, which you should have received from your breeder. Your vet is a great source of canine health information, so be sure to ask questions and take notes. Creating a health journal for your puppy will make a handy reference for his wellness and any future health problems that may arise.

MEETING THE FAMILY

Your Field Spaniel's homecoming is an exciting time for all members of the family, and it's only natural that everyone will be eager to meet him, pet him and play with him. However, for the puppy's sake, it's best to make these initial family meetings as uneventful as possible so that the pup is not over-

PUPPY SHOTS

Puppies are born with natural antibodies that protect them from most canine diseases. They receive more antibodies from the colostrum in their mother's milk. These immunities wear off, however, and must be replaced through a series of vaccines. Puppy shots are given at 3- to 4-week intervals starting at 6 to 8 weeks of age through 16 to 20 weeks of age. Booster shots are given around one year of age, and every one to three years thereafter.

Provide your Field Spaniel with clean water in his own bowl so that he's not tempted to quench his thirst elsewhere.

whelmed with too much too soon. Remember, he has just left his dam and his littermates and is away from the breeder's home for the first time. Despite his fuzzy wagging tail, he is still apprehensive and wondering where he is and who all these strange humans are. It's best to let him explore on his own and meet the family members as he feels comfortable. Let him investigate all of the new smells, sights and sounds at his own pace. Children should be especially careful to not get overly excited, use loud voices or hug the pup too tightly. Be calm, gentle and affectionate, and be ready to comfort him if he appears frightened or uneasy.

Be sure to show your puppy his new crate during this first day home. Toss a treat or two inside the crate; if he associates the crate with food, he will associate the crate with good things. If he is comfortable with the crate, you can offer him his first meal inside it. Leave the door ajar so he can wander in and out as he chooses.

FIRST NIGHT IN HIS NEW HOME

So much has happened in your Field Spaniel puppy's first day away from the breeder. He's had his first car ride to his new home. He's met his new human family and perhaps the other family pets. He has explored his new house and yard, at least those places where he is to be allowed during his first weeks at home. He may have visited his new veterinarian. He has eaten his first meal or two away from his dam and littermates. Surely that's enough to tire out an eight-week-old Field Spaniel pup…or so you hope!

It's bedtime. During the day, the pup investigated his crate, which is his new den and sleeping space, so it is not entirely strange to him. Line the crate with a soft

THE FIRST FAMILY MEETING

Your puppy's first day at home should be quiet and uneventful. Despite his wagging tail, he is still wondering where his mom and siblings are! Let him make friends with other members of the family on his own terms; don't overwhelm him. You have a lifetime ahead to get to know each other!

MEET AND MINGLE

Puppies need to meet people and see the world if they are to grow up confident and unafraid. Take your puppy with you on everyday outings and errands. On-lead walks around the neighborhood and to the park offer the pup good exposure to the goings-on of his new human world. Avoid areas frequented by other dogs until your puppy has had his full round of puppy shots; ask your vet when your pup will be properly protected. Arrange for your puppy to meet new people of all ages every week.

towel or blanket that he can snuggle into and gently place him into the crate for the night. Some breeders send home a piece of bedding from where the pup slept with his littermates, and those familiar scents are a great comfort for the puppy on his first night without his siblings.

He will probably whine or cry. The puppy is objecting to the confinement and the fact that he is alone for the first time. This can be a stressful time for you as well as for the pup. It's important that you remain strong and don't let the puppy out of his crate to comfort him. He will fall asleep eventually. If you release him, the puppy will learn that crying means "out" and will continue that habit. You are laying the groundwork for future habits. Some breeders find that soft music can soothe a crying pup and help him get to sleep.

SOCIALIZING YOUR PUPPY

The first 20 weeks of your Field Spaniel puppy's life are the most important of his entire lifetime. A properly socialized puppy will grow up to be a confident and stable adult who will be a pleasure to live with and a welcome addition to the neighborhood.

The importance of socialization cannot be overemphasized. Research on canine behavior has proven that puppies who are not exposed to new sights, sounds, people and animals during their first 20 weeks of life will grow up to be timid and fearful, even aggressive, and unable to flourish outside of their familiar home environment.

Socializing your puppy is not difficult and, in fact, will be a fun

Working Field Spaniels enjoy the protection of a weatherproof coat, necessary for the rigors of the hunt.

Your Field Spaniel puppy will not take long to acclimate to the comforts of home.

time for you both. Lead training goes hand in hand with socialization, so your puppy will be learning how to walk on a lead at the same time that he's meeting the neighborhood. Because the Field Spaniel is such a terrific breed, everyone will enjoy meeting "the new kid on the block." Take him for short walks to the park and to other dog-friendly places where he will encounter new people, especially children. Puppies automatically recognize children as "little people" and are drawn to play with them. Just make sure that you supervise these meetings and that the children do not get too rough or encourage him to play too hard. An overzealous pup can often nip too hard, frightening the child and in turn making the puppy overly excited. A bad experience in puppyhood can impact a dog for life, so a pup that has a negative experience with a child may grow up to be shy or even aggressive around children.

Take your puppy along on your daily errands. Puppies are natural "people magnets," and most people who see your pup will want to pet him. All of these encounters will help to mold him into a confident adult dog. Likewise, you will soon feel like a confident, responsible dog owner, rightly proud of your mannerly Field Spaniel.

Be especially careful of your puppy's encounters and experiences during the eight-to-ten-week-old period, which is also called the

FIRST CAR RIDE

The ride to your home from the breeder might just be your puppy's first automobile experience, and you should make every effort to keep him comfortable and secure. Bring a large towel or small blanket for the puppy to lie on during the trip and an extra towel in case the pup gets carsick or has a potty accident. It's best to have another person with you to hold the puppy in his lap. Most puppies will fall fast asleep from the rolling motion of the car. If the ride is lengthy, you may have to stop so that the puppy can relieve himself, so be sure to bring a leash and collar for those stops. Avoid rest areas for potty trips, since those are frequented by many dogs, who may carry parasites or disease. It's better to stop at grassy areas near gas stations or shopping centers to prevent unhealthy exposure for your pup.

THE FAMILY TREE

Your puppy's pedigree is his family tree. Just as a child may resemble his parents and grandparents, so too will a puppy reflect the qualities, good and bad, of his ancestors, especially those in the first two generations. Therefore it's important to know as much as possible about a puppy's immediate relatives. Reputable and experienced breeders should be able to explain the pedigree and why they chose to breed from the particular dogs they used.

"fear period." This is a serious imprinting period, and all contact during this time should be gentle and positive. A frightening or negative event could leave a permanent impression that could affect his future behavior if a similar situation arises.

Also make sure that your puppy has received his first and second rounds of vaccinations before you expose him to other dogs or bring him to places that other dogs may frequent. Avoid dog parks and other strange-dog areas until your vet assures you that your puppy is fully immunized and resistant to the diseases that can be passed between canines. Discuss safe socialization with your breeder, as some breeders recommend socializing the puppy even before he has received all of his inoculations.

LEADER OF THE PUPPY'S PACK

Like other canines, your puppy needs an authority figure, someone he can look up to and regard as the leader of his "pack." His first pack leader was his dam, who taught him to be polite and not chew too hard on her ears or nip at her muzzle. He learned those same lessons from his littermates. If he played too rough, they cried in pain and stopped the game, which sent an important message to the rowdy puppy.

As puppies play together, they are also struggling to determine who will be the boss. Being pack animals, dogs need someone to be in charge. If a litter of puppies remained together beyond puppyhood, one of the pups would emerge as the strongest one, the one who calls the shots.

Once your puppy leaves the pack, he will look intuitively for a new leader. If he does not recog-

At nine-and-a-half weeks old, this puppy has a beautiful Field expression accented by gentle brown eyes and framed with long, silky ears.

This curious Field puppy is not shy about introducing himself to a new friend.

nize you as that leader, he will try to assume that position for himself. Of course, it is hard to imagine your adorable Field Spaniel puppy trying to be in charge when he is so small and seemingly helpless. You must remember that these are natural canine instincts. Do not cave in and allow your pup to get the upper "paw"!

Just as socialization is so important during these first 20 weeks, so too is your puppy's early education. He was born without any bad habits. He does not know what is good or bad behavior. If he does things like nipping and digging, it's because he is having fun and doesn't know that humans consider these things as "bad." It's your job to teach him proper puppy manners, and this is the best time to accomplish that...before he has developed bad habits, since it is much more difficult to "unlearn" or correct unacceptable learned behavior than to teach good behavior from the start.

Make sure that all members of the family understand the importance of being consistent when training their new puppy. If you tell the puppy to stay off the sofa and your daughter allows him to cuddle on the couch to watch her favorite television show, your pup will be confused about what he is and is not allowed to do. Have a family conference before your pup comes home so that everyone understands the basic principles of puppy training and the rules you have set forth for the pup, and agrees to follow them.

The old saying that "an ounce of prevention is worth a pound of cure" is especially true when it comes to puppies. It is much easier to prevent inappropriate behavior than it is to change it. It's also easier and less stressful for the

HAPPY PUPPIES COME RUNNING

Never call your puppy (or adult dog) to come to you and then scold him or discipline him when he gets there. He will make a natural association between coming to you and being scolded, and he will think he was a bad dog for coming to you. He will then be reluctant to come whenever he is called. Always praise your puppy every time he comes to you.

ESTABLISH A ROUTINE

Routine is very important to a puppy's learning environment. To facilitate house-training, use the same exit/entrance door for potty trips and always take the puppy to the same place in the yard. The same principle of consistency applies to all other aspects of puppy training.

pup, since it will keep discipline to a minimum and create a more positive learning environment for him. That, in turn, will also be easier on you!

Here are a few commonsense tips to keep your belongings safe and your puppy out of trouble:

- Keep your closet doors closed and your shoes, socks and other apparel off the floor so your puppy can't get at them.
- Keep a secure lid on the trash container or put the trash where your puppy can't dig into it. He can't damage what he can't reach!
- Supervise your puppy at all times to make sure he is not getting into mischief. If he starts to chew the corner of the rug, you can distract him instantly by tossing a toy for him to fetch. You also will be able to whisk him outside when you notice that he is about to piddle on the carpet. If you can't see your puppy, you can't teach or correct his behavior.

SOLVING PUPPY PROBLEMS

Chewing and Nipping

Nipping at fingers and toes is normal puppy behavior. Chewing is also the way that puppies investigate their surroundings. However, you will have to teach your puppy that chewing anything other than his toys is not acceptable. That won't happen overnight and at times puppy teeth will test your patience. However, if you allow nipping and chewing to continue, just think about the damage that a mature Field Spaniel can do with a full set of adult teeth.

Whenever your puppy nips your hand or fingers, cry out "Ouch!" in a loud voice, which should startle your puppy and stop him from nipping, even if only for a moment. Immediately distract him by offering a small treat or an

Fields of all ages are happy to tell the world how much they enjoy playtime.

Field Spaniels are intelligent and hard-working dogs. They are capable of learning many things, and they enjoy the challenges of training.

appropriate toy for him to chew instead (which means having chew toys and puppy treats handy or in your pockets at all times). Praise him when he takes the toy and tell him what a good fellow he is. Praise is just as or even more important in puppy training as discipline and correction.

Puppies also tend to nip at children more often than adults, since they perceive little ones to be more vulnerable and more similar to their littermates. Teach your children appropriate responses to nipping behavior. If they are unable to handle it themselves, you may have to intervene. Puppy nips can be quite painful and a child's frightened reaction will only encourage a puppy to nip harder, which is a natural canine response. As with all other puppy situations, interaction between your Field Spaniel puppy and children should be supervised.

Chewing on objects, not just family members' fingers and ankles, is also normal canine behavior that can be especially tedious (for the owner, not the pup) during the teething period when the puppy's adult teeth are coming in. At this stage, chewing just plain feels good. Furniture legs and cabinet corners are common puppy favorites. Shoes and other personal items also taste pretty good to a pup.

The best solution is, once again, prevention. If you value something, keep it tucked away and out of reach. You can't hide your dining-room table in a closet, but you can try to deflect the chewing by applying a bitter product made just to deter dogs from chewing. This spray-on substance is vile-tasting, although safe for dogs, and most puppies will avoid the forbidden object after one tiny taste. You also can apply the product to your leather leash if the puppy tries to chew on his lead during leash-training sessions.

Keep a ready supply of safe chews handy to offer to your Field Spaniel as a distraction when he starts to chew on something that's a "no-no." Remember, at this tender age he does not yet know what is permitted or forbidden, so you have to be "on call" every minute he's awake and on the prowl.

You may lose a treasure or two during puppy's growing-up period, and the furniture could sustain a nasty nick or two. These can be trying times, so be prepared for those inevitable accidents and comfort yourself in knowing that this too shall pass.

Jumping Up

Although Field Spaniel pups are not known to be notorious jumpers, they are still puppies after all, and puppies jump up…on you, your guests, your counters and your furniture. Just another normal part of growing up, and

Field pups are curious creatures who like to investigate every corner and crevice.

one you need to meet head-on before it becomes an ingrained habit.

The key to jump correction is consistency. You cannot correct your Field Spaniel for jumping up on you today, then allow it to happen tomorrow by greeting him with hugs and kisses. As you have learned by now, consistency is critical to all puppy lessons.

For starters, try turning your back as soon as the puppy jumps. Jumping up is a means of gaining your attention and, if the pup can't see your face, he may get discouraged and learn that he loses eye contact with his beloved master when he jumps up.

Leash corrections also work, and most puppies respond well to a leash tug if they jump. Grasp the leash close to the puppy's collar and give a quick tug downward, using the command "Off." Do not use the word "Down," since "Down" is used to teach the puppy to lie down, which is a separate action that he will learn during his education in the basic commands. As soon as the puppy has backed off, tell him to sit and immediately praise him for doing so. This will take many repetitions and won't be accomplished quickly, so don't get discouraged or give up; you must be even more persistent than your puppy.

A second method used for jump correction is the spritzer bottle. Fill a spray bottle with water mixed with a bit of lemon juice or vinegar. As soon as puppy jumps, command him "Off" and spritz him with the water mixture. Of course, that means having the spray bottle handy whenever or wherever jumping usually happens.

Yet a third method to discourage jumping is grasping the puppy's paws and holding them gently but firmly until he struggles to get away. Wait a brief moment or two, then release his paws and give him a command to sit. He should eventually learn that jumping gets him into an uncomfortable predicament.

Children are major victims of puppy jumping, since puppies view little people as ready targets for jumping up as well as nipping. If your children (or their friends) are unable to dispense jump corrections, you will have to intervene and handle it for them.

Important to prevention is also knowing what you should not do. Never kick your Field Spaniel (for any reason, not just for jumping) or knock him in the chest with your knee. That maneuver could actually harm your puppy. Vets can tell you stories about puppies who suffered broken bones after being banged about when they jumped up.

Puppy Whining

Puppies often cry and whine, just as infants and little children do. It's their way of telling us that they are lonely or in need of attention. Your puppy will miss his littermates and will feel insecure when he is left alone. You may be out of the house or just in another room, but he will still feel alone. During these times, the puppy's crate should be his personal comfort station, a place all his own where he can feel safe and secure. Once he learns that being alone is okay and not something to be feared, he will settle down without crying or objecting. You might want to leave a radio on while he is crated, as the sound of human voices can be soothing and will give the impression that people are around.

Give your puppy a favorite cuddly toy or chew toy to entertain him whenever he is crated. You will both be happier: the puppy because he is safe in his den and you because he is quiet, safe and not getting into puppy escapades that can wreak havoc in your house or cause him danger.

To make sure that your puppy will always view his crate as a safe and cozy place, never, ever, use the crate as punishment. That's the best way to turn the crate into a negative place that the pup will want to avoid. Sure, you can use the crate for your own peace of mind if your puppy is getting into trouble and needs some "time out." Just don't let him know that! Never scold the pup and immediately place him into the crate. Count to ten, give him a couple of hugs and maybe a treat, then scoot him into his crate.

It's also important not to make a big fuss when he is released from the crate. That will make getting out of the crate more appealing than being in the crate, which is just the opposite of what you are trying to achieve.

A SMILE'S WORTH A MILE

Don't embark on your puppy's training course when you're not in the mood. Never train your puppy if you're feeling grouchy or impatient with him. Subjecting your puppy to your bad mood is a bad move. Your pup will sense your negative attitude, and neither of you will enjoy the session or have any measure of success. Always begin and end your training sessions on a happy note.

PROPER CARE OF YOUR
FIELD SPANIEL

Adding a Field Spaniel to your household means adding a new family member who will need your care each and every day. When your Field Spaniel pup first comes home, you will start a routine with him so that, as he grows up, your dog will have a daily schedule just as you do. The aspects of your dog's daily care will likewise become regular parts of your day, so you'll both have a new schedule. Dogs learn by consistency and thrive on routine: regular times for meals, exercise, grooming and potty trips are just as important for your dog as they are for you! Your dog's schedule will depend much on your family's daily routine, but remember that you now have a new member of the family who is part of your day every day.

FEEDING

Feeding your dog the best diet is based on various factors, including age, activity level, overall condition and size of breed. When you visit the breeder, he will share with you his advice about the proper diet for your dog based on his experience with the breed and the foods with which he has had success. Likewise, your vet will be a helpful source of advice throughout the dog's life and will aid you in planning a diet for optimal health.

Feeding the Puppy

Of course, your pup's very first food will be his dam's milk. There may be special situations in which pups fail to nurse, necessitating that the breeder hand-feed them with a formula,

VARIETY IS THE SPICE

Although dog-food manufacturers contend that dogs don't like variety in their diets, studies show quite the opposite to be true. Dogs would much rather vary their meals than eat the same old chow day in and day out. Dry kibble is no more exciting for a dog than the same bowl of bran flakes would be for you. Fortunately, there are dozens of varieties available on the market, and your dog will likely show preference for certain flavors over others. A word of warning: don't offer too many variations or you'll develop a fussy eater who only prefers chopped beef fillet and asparagus tips every night.

but for the most part pups spend the first weeks of life nursing from their dam. The breeder weans the pups by gradually introducing solid foods and decreasing the milk meals. Pups may even start themselves off on the weaning process, albeit inadvertently, if they snatch bites from their mom's food bowl.

DIET DON'TS

- Got milk? Don't give it to your dog! Dogs cannot tolerate large quantities of cows' milk, as they do not have the enzymes to digest lactose.
- You may have heard of dog owners who add raw eggs to their dogs' food for a shiny coat or to make the food more palatable, but consumption of raw eggs too often can cause a deficiency of the vitamin biotin.
- Avoid feeding table scraps, as they will upset the balance of the dog's complete food. Additionally, fatty or highly seasoned foods can cause upset canine stomachs.
- Do not offer raw meat to your dog. Raw meat can contain parasites; it also is high in fat.
- Vitamin A toxicity in dogs can be caused by too much raw liver, especially if the dog already gets enough vitamin A in his balanced diet, which should be the case.
- Bones like chicken, pork chop and other soft bones are not suitable, as they easily splinter.

A Field puppy's feeding differs from that of many other breeds, as puppy food is not the optimal way to feed for proper Field Spaniel growth.

By the time the pups are ready for new homes, they are fully weaned and eating a good puppy food. As a new owner, you may be thinking, "Great! The breeder has taken care of the hard part." Not so fast.

Vets often recommend that puppies be maintained on a food formulated for puppies until one year of age. This is *not* ideal for Field Spaniels. Food formulated specifically for puppies often encourages a rate of growth in body mass (weight) that outpaces the strength of musculature and other soft-tissue support structures. The result is that the front assembly of the dog suffers. Feed your Field pup a good-quality adult dog food. The Field Spaniel puppy should be lean. Like the gawky human adolescent, the appearance should portend that there is much more to come as the frame slowly fills out with maturity.

The Field is a slow-maturing breed, with full maturity not seen

SUPPLEMENTING YOUR FIELD SPANIEL'S DIET

While excessive supplementation is not recommended, there are some supplements commonly used by Field Spaniel fanciers. Among them are:

Kelp: a supplement to enhance overall immune-system function and improve coat that is used by a number of fanciers.

Vitamin C: this water-soluble vitamin is often used during major growth phases, typically until the puppy reaches two years of age.

Omega fatty-acid supplements: these oils are often useful, particularly with liver-colored coats, which tend to be somewhat drier and less glossy than the black haircoat.

Other supplements used vary widely, according to individual preferences of breeders. It is best to consult with the breeder of your puppy and follow his feeding instructions.

until three years of age. While the one-year-old Field Spaniel may have his full height, substantial changes can and do occur in body substance and coat. The Field Spaniel is not a small spaniel. Puppies that mature too quickly may not develop the overall size and substance typical for the breed.

Many Field Spaniel owners have had considerable success with natural diets for their companions following the recommendations of any one of several reputable authors to assure that the diet is balanced. Some fanciers also believe strongly in using dog dishes that are raised off the floor. Bowl stands are available from most well-stocked pet shops. These stands are thought to be beneficial in providing a more natural feeding position as well as to make the puppy "stretch" up and avoid bearing down on the front pasterns. It is always wise to consult the breeder of your puppy as well as your vet about specific feeding practices such as this.

Because of a young pup's small body and accordingly small digestive system, his daily portion will be divided up into small meals throughout the day. This can mean starting off with three or more meals a day and decreasing the number of meals as the pup matures. For the adult, it is generally thought that dividing the day's food into two meals on a morning/evening schedule is healthier for the dog's digestion than one large daily portion.

Regarding the feeding schedule, feeding the pup at the same times and in the same place each day is important for both housebreaking purposes and establishing the dog's everyday routine. As for the amount to feed, growing puppies generally need proportionately more food per body weight than their adult counterparts, but a pup should never be allowed to gain excess weight. Dogs of all ages should be kept in proper body condition, but extra weight can strain a pup's developing frame, causing skeletal problems.

Watch your pup's weight as he grows and, if the recommended amounts seem to be too much or too little for your pup, consult the vet about appropriate dietary changes. Keep in mind that treats, although small, can quickly add up throughout the day, contributing unnecessary calories. Treats are fine when used prudently; opt for dog treats specially formulated to be healthy or for nutritious snacks like small pieces of cheese or cooked chicken.

Puppies get the best start in life by nursing from mom, whose milk contains antibody-rich colostrum to protect them and build their immune systems.

NOT HUNGRY?

No dog in his right mind would turn down his dinner, would he? If you notice that your dog has lost interest in his food, there could be any number of causes. Dental problems are a common cause of appetite loss, one that is often overlooked. If your dog has a toothache, a loose tooth or sore gums from infection, chances are it doesn't feel so good to chew. Think about when you've had a toothache! If your dog does not approach the food bowl with his usual enthusiasm, look inside his mouth for signs of a problem. Whatever the cause, you'll want to consult your vet so that your chow hound can get back to his happy, hungry self as soon as possible.

Feeding the Adult Dog

For the adult (meaning physically mature) dog, feeding properly is about maintenance, not growth. Again, correct weight is a concern. Your dog should appear fit and should have an evident "waist." His ribs should not be protruding (a sign of being underweight), but they should be

This happy young Field is ready to dig in!

covered by only a slight layer of fat. Under normal circumstances, an adult dog can be maintained fairly easily with a high-quality nutritionally complete adult-formula food.

Factor treats into your dog's overall daily caloric intake, and avoid offering table scraps. Not only are certain "people foods," like chocolate, nuts, raisins, grapes, onions and significant quantities of garlic, toxic to dogs but feeding from your plate also encourages begging and overeating. Overweight dogs are more prone to health problems. Research has even shown that obesity takes years off a dog's life. With that in mind, resist the urge to overfeed and over-treat. Don't make unnecessary additions to your dog's diet, whether with tidbits or with extra vitamins and minerals.

The amount of food needed for proper maintenance will vary depending on the individual dog's activity level, but you will be able to tell whether the daily portions are keeping him in good shape. With the wide variety of good complete foods available, choosing what to feed is largely a matter of personal preference. Just

SWITCHING FOODS

There are certain times in a dog's life when you may need to switch his food; for example, you might switch your older dog from adult to senior-dog food. Additionally, you may decide to feed your pup a different type of food from what he received from the breeder, and there may be "emergency" situations in which you can't find your dog's normal brand and have to offer something else temporarily. Anytime a change is made, for whatever reason, the switch must be done gradually. You don't want to upset the dog's stomach or end up with a picky eater who refuses to eat something new. A tried-and-true approach is, over the course of about a week, to mix a little of the new food in with the old, increasing the proportion of new to old as the days progress. At the end of the week, you'll be feeding his regular portions of the new food, and he will barely notice the change.

as with the puppy, the adult dog should have consistency in his mealtimes and feeding place. In addition to a consistent routine, regular mealtimes also allow the owner to see how much his dog is eating. If the dog seems never to be satisfied or, likewise, becomes uninterested in his food, the owner will know right away that something is wrong and can consult the vet.

Diets for the Aging Dog

What does aging have to do with your dog's diet? No, he won't get a discount at the local diner's early-bird special, but he may require some dietary changes to accommodate the changes that come along with increased age. Discuss with your vet whether you need to switch to a higher-protein or senior-formulated food or whether your current adult-dog food contains sufficient nutrition for the senior.

The Field Spaniel is a long-lived breed with an average lifespan of 14 years, typically ranging between 12–16 years. The shift, if any, from adult to senior dog food should be made based on the needs of the individual animal rather than according to age. Senior Fields may often continue to be fed regular adult dog food with no ill effects. Others, particularly those who are less active or with weight-control problems, may do better on a senior food that has fewer calories. For seniors with specific medical problems, special diets are often needed.

Watching the dog's weight remains essential, even more so in the senior stage of life. Older dogs

QUENCHING HIS THIRST

Is your dog drinking more than normal and trying to lap up everything in sight? Excessive drinking has many different causes. Obvious causes for a dog's being thirstier than usual are hot weather and vigorous exercise. However, if your dog is drinking more for no apparent reason, you could have cause for concern. Serious conditions like kidney or liver disease, diabetes and various types of hormonal problems can all be indicated by excessive drinking. If you notice your dog's being excessively thirsty, contact your vet at once. Hopefully there will be a simpler explanation, but the earlier a serious problem is detected, the sooner it can be treated, with a better rate of cure.

are already more vulnerable to illness, and obesity only contributes to their susceptibility to problems.

DON'T FORGET THE WATER!

For a dog, it's always time for a drink! Regardless of what type of food he eats, there's no doubt that he needs plenty of water. Fresh cold water, in a clean bowl, should be freely available to your dog at all times. There are special circumstances, such as during puppy housebreaking, when you will want to monitor your pup's water intake so that you will be able to predict when he will need to relieve himself, but water must be available to him nonetheless. Water is essential for hydration and proper body function just as it is in humans.

PUPPY STEPS

Puppies are brimming with activity and enthusiasm. It seems that they can play all day and night without tiring, but don't overdo your puppy's exercise regimen. Easy does it for the puppy's first six to nine months. Keep walks brief and don't let the puppy engage in stressful jumping games. The puppy frame is delicate, and too much exercise during those critical growing months can cause injury to his bone structure, ligaments and musculature. Save his first jog for his first birthday!

You will get to know how much your dog typically drinks in a day. Of course, in the heat or if exercising vigorously, he will be more thirsty and will drink more. However, if he begins to drink noticeably more water for no apparent reason, this could signal any of various problems, and you are advised to consult your vet.

Water is the best drink for dogs. Some owners are tempted to give milk from time to time or to moisten dry food with milk, but dogs do not have the enzymes necessary to digest the lactose in milk, which is much different from the milk that nursing puppies receive. Therefore stick with clean fresh water to quench your dog's thirst, and always have it readily available to him.

EXERCISE

The Field Spaniel's exercise needs vary greatly among individuals. Field Spaniels from lines bred for not only conformation but also working ability (hunting, obedience, agility, tracking) will typically need more exercise than those from lines bred primarily for the conformation show ring with less emphasis on performance. On the average, a couple of brisk 15- to 20-minute walks or sessions of throwing a tennis ball or retrieving a bumper in the yard are recommended. Creating a safe place for a Field Spaniel puppy to play freely, such as a fenced yard, is helpful to allow the puppy to exercise to the amount that the puppy requires. That being said, all Field Spaniels need *quality* exercise that includes interaction and playtime with their human companions; this is not a breed that will be content to be relegated to the yard on its own.

On that note, some precautions should be taken with a puppy's exercise. During his first year, when he is growing and developing, your Field Spaniel should not be subject to stressful activity that stresses his body. Short walks at a comfortable pace and play sessions in the yard are good for a growing pup, and his exercise can be increased as he grows up.

TWO'S COMPANY

One surefire method of increasing your adult dog's exercise plan is to adopt a second dog. If your dog is well socialized, he should take to his new canine pal in no time and soon the two will be giving each other lots of activity and exercise as they play, romp and explore together. Most owners agree that two dogs are hardly much more work than one. If you cannot afford a second dog, get together with a friend or neighbor who has a well-trained dog. Your dog will enjoy the company of a new four-legged playmate.

It's not hard to keep a Field Spaniel active, as there is so much that he enjoys doing.

For overweight dogs, dietary changes and activity will help the goal of weight loss. (Sound familiar?) While they should of course be encouraged to be active, remember not to overdo it, as the excess weight is already putting strain on his vital organs and bones. As for highly active dogs, some of them never seem to tire! They will enjoy time spent with their owners doing things together.

Regardless of your dog's condition and activity level, exercise offers benefits to all dogs and owners. Consider the fact that dogs who are kept active are more stimulated both physically and mentally, meaning that they are less likely to become bored and lapse into destructive behavior. Also consider the benefits of one-on-one time with your dog every day, continually strengthening the bond between the two of you.

Furthermore, exercising together will improve health and longevity for both of you. You both need exercise, and now you and your dog have a workout partner and motivator!

GROOMING THE FIELD SPANIEL

While grooming for the show ring has considerable variations from country to country, there are basic grooming regimens that are necessary for the overall health and well-being of the Field Spaniel as well as for the maintenance of the typical appearance. The basic grooming described here is for the household companion. Grooming for show may require a bit more to learn, and the breeder of your dog is often your very best source of information for learning the requirements of show grooming. Do not be surprised if local groomers have never seen a Field Spaniel!

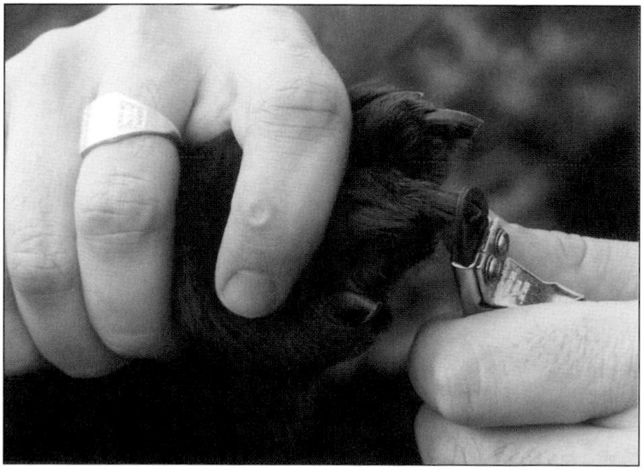

A dog does not always appreciate his pedicures but should learn to at least tolerate the routine.

Care of the Toenails

Field Spaniels generally have tough black toenails and the "quick" (vascular nail bed) is nearly impossible to see. Nails must be trimmed on a weekly basis, as nails that are too long may result in improper placement

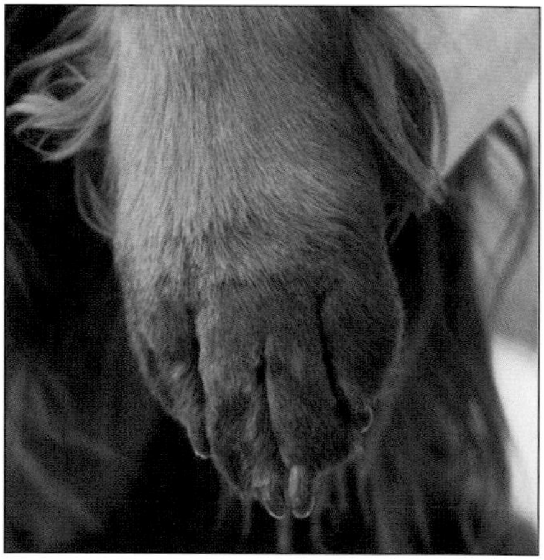

Field Spaniels have tough black toenails that require regular trimming and maintenance with tools made for dogs' nails.

of the foot as the nail hits the floor. A nail clipper is used to clip off the end of the nail, followed by using the nail file to smooth rough edges. Styptic powder is crucial to have nearby since with the difficulty of seeing where the nail bed lies, it is all too easy to cut a bit too close. As an alternative, a nail grinder may be used to shorten the nail and provide the smoothing effect of the file at the same time. Many dogs dislike nail cutting intensely. This may be avoided by routinely handling the feet at times apart from nail cutting and introducing the puppy to the regimen at an early age.

ORAL HEALTH

Routine care of the mouth is important to prevent tooth decay and gum disease. Weekly attention to brushing the teeth is helpful for maintaining the teeth in the best possible manner. While providing chew bones is helpful to naturally remove tartar build-up as the dog gnaws, this is often

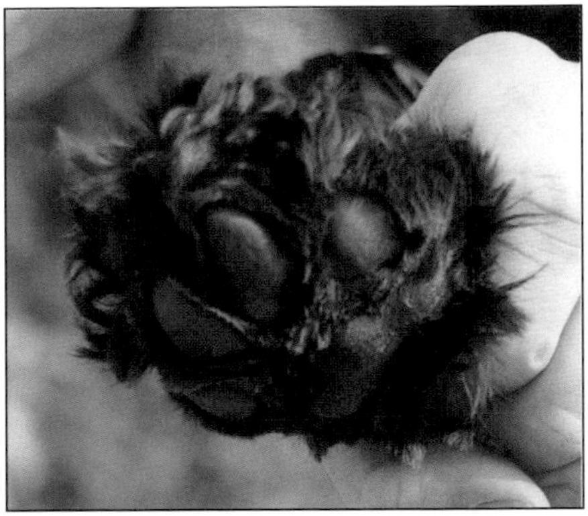

The untrimmed foot of a Field Spaniel.

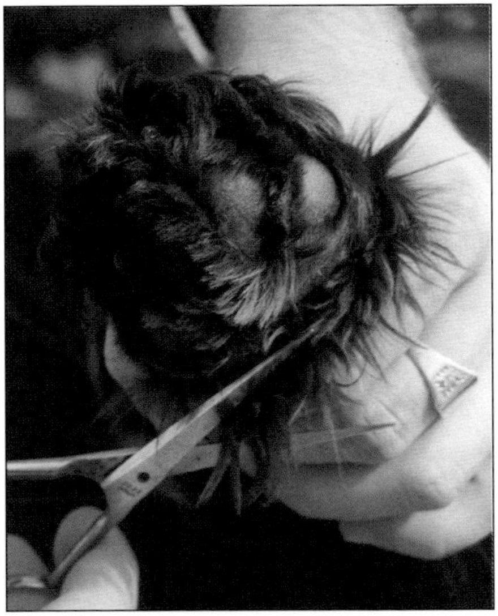

Excess hair should be scissored off for a tidy appearance and to keep the feet comfortable for the dog.

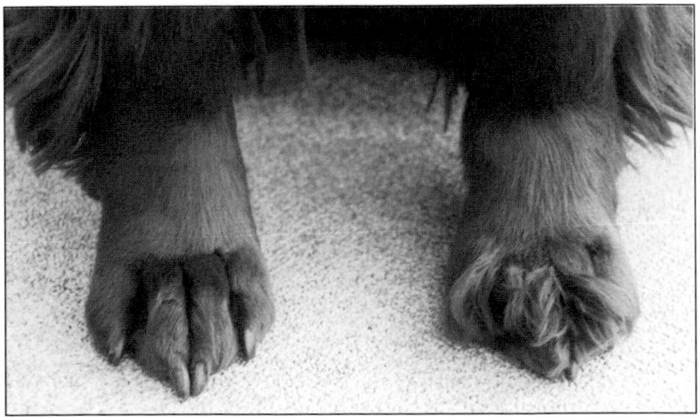

Compare the trimmed to the untrimmed foot. Also notice the neatly trimmed nails.

GROOMING EQUIPMENT FOR YOUR FIELD SPANIEL

- Nail clipper and nail file or nail grinder
- Styptic powder
- Ear cleanser, powder or liquid as recommended by your veterinarian or breeder
- Cotton balls or wipes
- Soft toothbrush and canine-formula toothpaste
- Bristle brush (natural bristle style recommended)
- "Greyhound"-style comb
- Straight shears
- Stripping knife
- Shampoo formulated for canines
- Hand-held blow dryer
- Electric clipper with 7F blade (optional)
- Thinning shears (optional)
- Grooming spray for daily use (optional)
- Grooming table (optional)
- Coat conditioner for use after bathing (optional)
- SPF-rated sun protection spray for coat (optional)

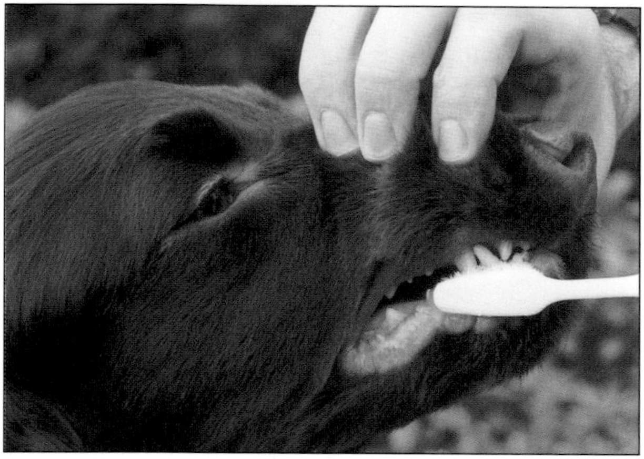

A frequently neglected aspect of grooming dogs is their teeth. Your Field Spaniel's teeth should be brushed at least once per week.

not sufficient. You can purchase a dog toothbrush and paste at your local pet shop or from your vet.

Tending to the Ears

The beautiful ears of the Field Spaniel that frame the face so well and contribute greatly to the soft spaniel expression do require routine care. Ears should be cleaned weekly using cotton wipes and a powder or liquid cleansing agent as recommended by your veterinarian or breeder. Do not be tempted to use a cotton swab instead of a cotton wipe. It is far too easy to probe too deeply with a swab and cause harm. Routine care of the ear goes a long way in preventing ear infections in this breed with pendulous ears as the weight and length of the ears effectively cloak the ear openings, thereby creating an ideal dark, moist environment for infection. It is recommended that the hair around the ear opening be shortened by plucking or by careful use of thinning shears to keep the ear as dry as possible, particularly for Field Spaniels who do a bit of swimming.

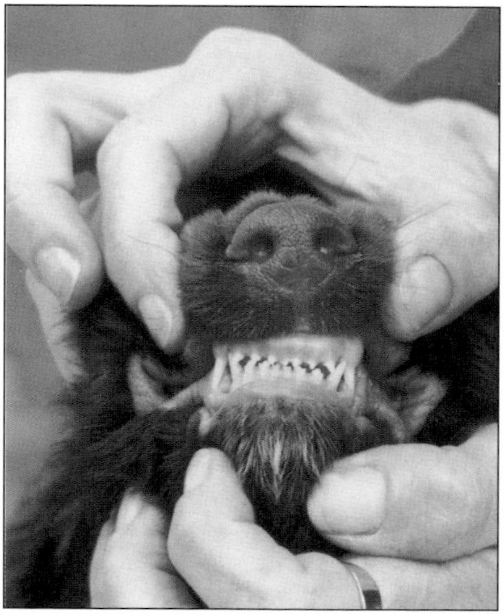

Pink gums and clean white teeth indicate good oral health. Check your Field's mouth often, as a healthy mouth is important for good overall health.

Bathing Your Field Spaniel

The frequency of bathing will depend greatly on the dog's activities as well as the coat of the dog. Some Field Spaniels have coats that are oilier than others, and these may begin to smell "doggy" more quickly. Therefore, if your Field Spaniel is a household companion and sleeps on your bed, you may wish to bathe your dog a bit more often! Fields who are shown are often bathed far more frequently, particularly during show season. On the average, a home companion will require bathing no more frequently than once a month, especially if routine coat care via thorough brushings is done.

When bathing your Field, cotton balls placed in the outer ears will prevent water from getting into the ear canals. Using tepid water, just warm to the touch, thoroughly wet the dog, beginning at the head and working toward the tail, and from the top of the head to the feet. Using a product made for dogs, not humans, apply shampoo as directed on the bottle, but avoid the face while doing so to prevent any irritation to the sensitive eyes. The face is easily cleaned using a damp face towel. There are many different shampoo formulations available, some of which are medicated for use with specific coat and skin problems. The mildest shampoo is often the best to avoid stripping the coat of essential oils, particularly in the liver-colored coats. After thoroughly lathering the dog, paying attention to leg, belly and ear feathering, thoroughly rinse him with tepid water. A spray device, such as used for showering, makes the job of wetting and rinsing the dog much easier. It is essential that all traces of shampoo be removed, as leaving any shampoo in the coat will attract dirt as well as potentially irritate the skin.

It is helpful to apply a coat conditioner after towel drying and before blow drying. Just as a conditioning rinse is helpful to styling your own hair without tangles, so it works with Field Spaniel feathering. Leave the conditioner on for a minute or two and then rinse it out (although some conditioning products do not require rinsing; check the directions). It then is essential to dry the haircoat. A hand-held blow dryer set on "low" works quite well. Take care to direct the airflow away from the face and to

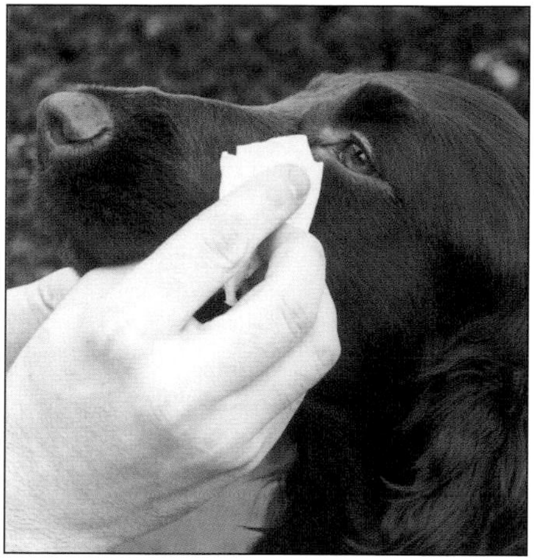

Tear stains can be removed with a cotton wipe and tear-stain-removal formula available from your local pet-supply shop.

Your Field Spaniel's ears should be cleaned weekly using cotton wipes and a cleansing agent made especially for dogs' ears.

maintain a safe distance between the dryer and the dog. When the dog is dry, use the bristle brush for the body coat and the comb to smooth out the feathering.

Brushing and Combing

Many Field Spaniels really enjoy spending time with their owners and the brush and comb! After all, it is a time when your dog has your undivided attention, and regular grooming can be very relaxing for both you and your dog. On at least a weekly basis, use the bristle brush, starting at the head and working toward the tail, always going with the lie of the hair. Avoid brushing the facial area; use a barely damp washcloth to groom this area, again always following the lie of the hair. Brushing removes dead hair and, when done with regularity, you will see far less shedding in the form of fluff-balls of dog hair drifting into corners! A conditioning grooming spray may

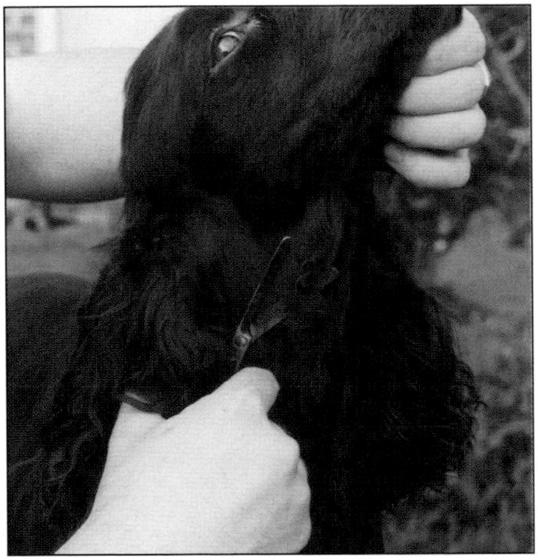

Thinning shears are used here to blend the hair on the neck area.

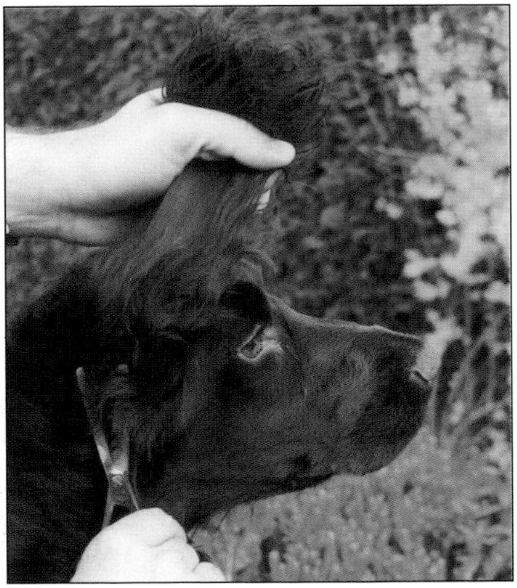

Shears are used carefully to shorten hair around the ear opening.

be used during brushing, as this helps to prevent coat damage and breakage that can occur when brushing or combing a completely dry coat.

Following brushing, use the comb for the feathering on the ears, legs and belly area. Gently work out any tangles that might be present to avoid any discomfort to your dog. If needed, depending on how much time your Field Spaniel spends outdoors, a sunscreen spray is helpful to apply as a final mist to prevent bleaching of the coat, which is particularly a problem for the liver coat color.

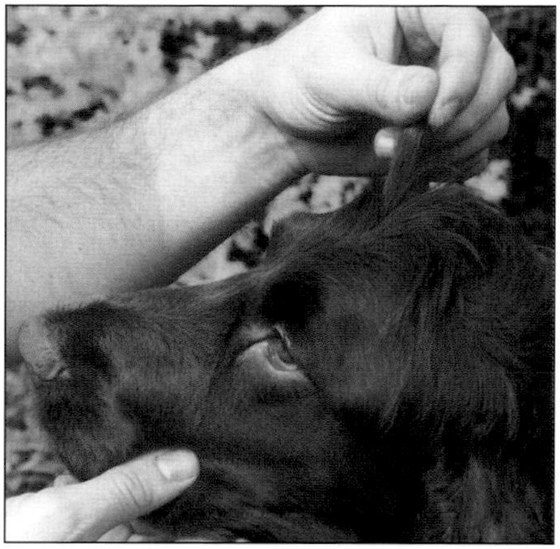

Hand stripping requires time to learn and practice to master.

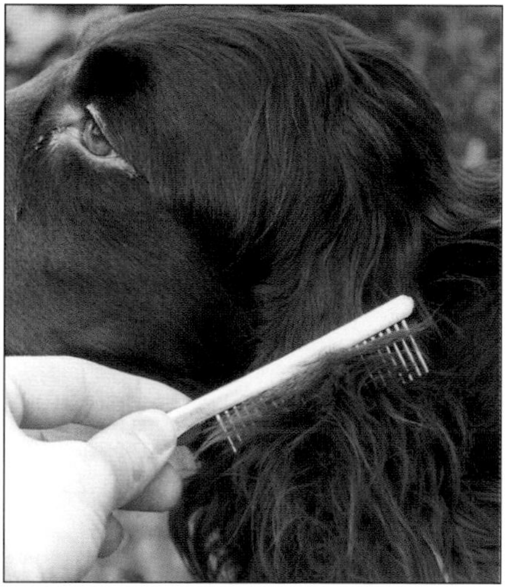

Following brushing, use the comb for the feathering on the ears.

The tail needs attention, too, and is tidied up with shears.

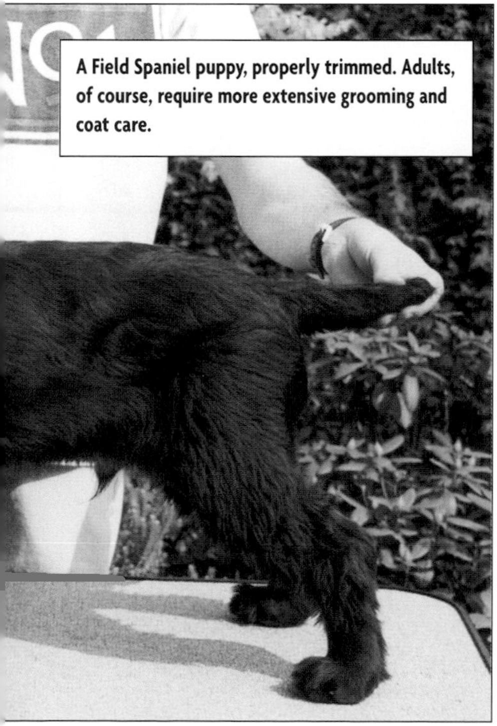

A Field Spaniel puppy, properly trimmed. Adults, of course, require more extensive grooming and coat care.

Trimming the Field's Coat

Neatening up the haircoat is helpful to maintain typical Field Spaniel appearance, whether the dog is a household companion or show dog. Trimming, even for the show ring, should only enhance the natural appearance of the dog. The choice of tools to use for trimming the haircoat varies considerably. It is safe to say that the stripping knife is utilized worldwide to remove dead coat as well as to blend coat or remove excessive length, while the straight shears are used to shorten the hair on the backs of the rear legs from hock to ground. The straight shears should also be carefully used to trim hair from the footpads so that the dog is not walking on hair and thereby losing the natural traction supplied by the pad.

Hair on the dog's hind legs is usually trimmed below the hock. The AKC standard states: "Pasterns have clean outlines to ground."

Untrimmed (left) versus trimmed (right) hind legs.

In general, the hair on the upper one-third of the outer ear is shortened to enhance the appearance of the set of the ear, allowing the ear to gracefully frame the face. This may be accomplished by use of the stripping knife, used

The Field Spaniel head trimmed on only one side to show the difference before and after trimming.

to blend the hair to lie flat and thereby create a gradual transition of the hair from skull to ear to neck, although fanciers in the US will often use an electric clipper with a #10 blade. Hair from the lower jaw area (an area about two finger-breadths above the prosternum of the chest) may also be shortened with a stripping knife to enhance the neckline of the dog. Again, the key is to remove just enough hair to neaten the appearance and blend well into the longer body coat.

Excessive facial hair may be carefully stripped by use of a small stripping knife created expressly for that purpose. Though in the United States and Canada an electric clipper with a 7F blade and/or thinning shears are often used for the ears, face and throat, this is not considered an ideal way to shorten the hair in many other countries where use of the electric clipper is particularly frowned upon as creating an artificial appearance.

In all countries, the stripping knife is the preferred tool to use on the body coat. An electric clipper or thinning shears should never be applied to the body coat, as to do so will often ruin the proper texture of the coat. As an alternative to the stripping knife, hand plucking of the body coat may also be done. Though this is very time-consuming and can take a bit of practice to master, it results in enhancing the coat to produce the best possible texture.

IDENTIFICATION AND TRAVEL

ID FOR YOUR DOG

You love your Field Spaniel and want to keep him safe. Of course you take every precaution to prevent his escaping from the yard or becoming lost or stolen. You have a sturdy high fence and you

SCOOTING HIS BOTTOM

Here's a doggy problem that many owners tend to neglect. If your dog is scooting his rear end around the carpet, he probably is experiencing anal-sac impaction or blockage. The anal sacs are the two grape-sized glands on either side of the dog's vent. The dog cannot empty these glands, which become filled with a foul-smelling material. The dog may attempt to lick the area to relieve the pressure. He may also rub his anus on your walls, furniture or floors.

Don't neglect your dog's rear end during grooming sessions. By squeezing both sides of the anus with a soft cloth, you can express some of the material in the sacs. If the material is pasty and thick, you likely will need the assistance of a veterinarian. Vets know how to express the glands and can show you how to do it correctly without hurting the dog or spraying yourself with the unpleasant liquid.

PET OR STRAY?

Besides the obvious benefit of providing your contact information to whoever finds your lost dog, an ID tag makes your dog more approachable and more likely to be recovered. A strange dog wandering the neighborhood without a collar and tags will look like a stray, while the collar and tags indicate that the dog is someone's pet. Even if the ID tags become detached from the collar, the collar alone will make a person more likely to pick up the dog.

always keep your dog on lead when out and about in public places. If your dog is not properly identified, however, you are overlooking a major aspect of his safety. We hope to never be in a situation where our dog is missing, but we should practice prevention in the unfortunate case that this happens; identification greatly increases the chances of your dog's being returned to you.

There are several ways to identify your dog. First, the traditional dog tag should be a staple in your dog's wardrobe, attached to his everyday collar. Tags can be made of sturdy plastic and various metals and should include your contact information so that a person who finds the dog can get in touch with you right away to arrange his return. Many people today enjoy the wide range of decorative tags available, so have fun and create a tag to match your dog's personality. Of course, it is important that the tag stays on the collar, so have a secure "O" ring attachment; you also can explore the type of tag that slides right onto the collar.

In addition to the ID tag, which every dog should wear even if identified by another method, two other forms of identification have become popular: microchipping and tattooing. In microchipping, a tiny scannable chip is painlessly inserted under the dog's skin. The number is registered to you so that, if your lost dog turns up at a clinic or shelter, the chip can be scanned to retrieve your contact information.

The advantage of the microchip is that it is a permanent form of ID, but there are some factors to consider. Several different companies make microchips, and not all are compatible with the others' scanning devices. It's best to find a company with a universal microchip that can be read by scanners made by other companies as well. It won't do any good to have the dog chipped if the information cannot be retrieved. Also, not every humane society, shelter and clinic is equipped with a scanner, although more and more facilities are equipping themselves. In fact, many shelters microchip dogs that they adopt out to new homes.

In the US, there are five or six major microchip manufacturers as well as a few databases, such as the American Kennel Club's Companion Animal Recovery unit and HomeAgain™ Companion Animal Retrieval System (Schering-Plough). In the UK, The Kennel Club is affiliated with the National Pet Register, operated by Wood Green Animal Shelters.

Because the microchip is not visible to the eye, the dog must wear a tag that states that he is microchipped so that whoever picks him up will know to have him scanned. This tag usually also contains the microchip registry's name and phone number and the dog's microchip ID number. He of course also should have a tag with your contact information in case his microchip information cannot be retrieved. Humane societies and veterinary clinics offer microchipping service, which is usually very affordable.

Though less popular than microchipping, tattooing is another permanent method of ID for dogs. Most vets perform this service, and there are also clinics that perform dog tattooing. This is also an affordable procedure and one that will not cause much discomfort for the dog. It is best to put the tattoo in a visible area, such as the underside of the ear flap, to deter theft. It is sad to say that there are cases of dogs' being stolen and sold to research laboratories, but such laboratories will not accept tattooed dogs.

To ensure that the tattoo is effective in aiding your dog's return to you, the tattoo number must be registered with a national organization. That way, when someone finds a tattooed dog, a phone call to the registry will quickly match the dog with his owner.

FEEDING IN HOT WEATHER

Even the most dedicated chow hound may have less of an appetite when the weather is hot or humid. If your dog leaves more of his food behind than usual, adjust his portions until the weather and his appetite return to normal. Never leave the uneaten portion in the bowl, hoping he will return to finish it, because higher temperatures encourage food spoilage and bacterial growth.

Hit the Road

Car travel with your Field Spaniel may be limited to necessity only, such as trips to the vet, or you may bring your dog along almost everywhere you go. This will depend much on your individual dog and how he reacts to rides in the car. You can begin desensitizing your dog to car travel as a pup so that it's something that he's used to. Still, some dogs suffer from motion sickness. Your vet

A wire crate can be used in your home, your car and for safe confinement away from home, but air travel requires an approved hard-sided travel crate with adequate ventilation.

may prescribe a medication for this if trips in the car pose a problem for your dog. At the very least, you will need to get him to the vet, so he will need to tolerate these trips with the least amount of hassle possible.

Start taking your pup on short trips, maybe just around the block to start. If he is fine with short trips, lengthen your rides a little at a time. Start to take him on your errands or just for drives around town. By this time it will be easy to tell whether your dog is a born traveler or would prefer staying at home when you are on the road.

Of course, safety is a concern for dogs in the car. First, he must travel securely, not left loose to roam about the car where he could be injured or distract the driver. A young pup can be held by a passenger initially but should soon graduate to a travel crate, which can be the same crate he uses in the home. Other options include a car harness (like a seat belt for dogs) and partitioning the back of the car with a gate made for this purpose.

Bring along what you will need for the dog. He should wear his collar and ID tags, of course, and you should bring his leash, water (and food if a long trip) and clean-up materials for potty breaks and in case of motion sickness. Always keep your dog on his leash when you make stops, and never leave him alone in the car. Many a dog has died from the heat inside a closed car; this does not take much time at all. A dog

CAN I COME, TOO?

Your dog can accompany you most anywhere you go. A picnic in the park and the kids' Little League game are just two examples of outdoor events where dogs likely will be welcome. Of course, your dog will need to be kept on lead or safely crated in a well-ventilated crate. Bring along your "doggy bag" with all of the supplies you will need, like water, food or treats and a stash of plastic bags or other clean-up aids. Including your dog in the family activities is fun for all of you, providing excellent owner/dog quality time and new socialization opportunities.

left alone inside a car can also be a target for thieves.

Up, Up and Away!

Taking a trip by air does not mean that your dog cannot accompany you, it just means that you will have to be well informed and well prepared. The majority of dogs travel as checked cargo; only the smallest of breeds are allowed in the cabin with their owners. Your dog must travel in an airline-approved travel crate appropriate to his size so that he will be safe and comfortable during the flight. If the crate that you use at home does not meet the airline's specifications, you can purchase one from the airline or from your pet-supply store (making sure it is labeled as airline-approved).

It's best to have the crate in advance of your trip to give the dog time to get accustomed to it. You can put a familiar blanket and a favorite toy or two in the crate with the dog to make him feel at home and to keep him occupied. The crate should be lined with absorbent material for the trip, with bowls for food and water, and a portion of dry food, attached to the outside of the crate. The crate must be labeled with "Live Animal," your contact information, your itinerary, feeding instructions and a statement asserting that the dog was fed within a certain time frame of arrival at the airport (check with your airline). You will also have to provide proof of current vaccinations.

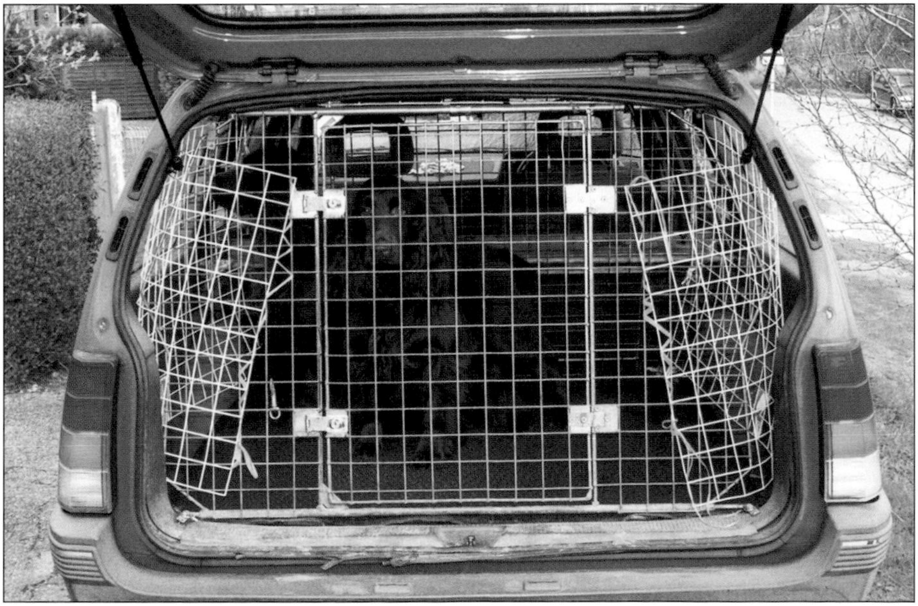

If you travel with your Field Spaniel fairly regularly, you can have your car outfitted with special safety gates to partition the rear section of the vehicle for your dog.

"Take us with you!" Fields love to be with their owners and to experience new adventures, so consider a dog-friendly vacation for *all* members of the family.

Again, advance planning is the key to smooth sailing in the skies. Make your reservations well ahead of time and know what restrictions your airline imposes: no travel during certain months, refusal of certain breeds, restrictions on certain destinations. Inform airline employees at each step of the way (check-in, boarding, etc.) that your pet is traveling as checked cargo. Major carriers are experienced with transporting animals, but every precaution you take helps the airline to help your pet have a safe flight.

Dog-Friendly Destinations

When planning vacations, a question that often arises is, "Who will watch the dog?" More and more families, however, are answering that question with, "We will!" With the rise in dog-friendly places to visit, the number of families who bring their dogs along on vacation is on the rise. A search online for dog-friendly vacation spots will turn up many choices, as well as resources for owners of canine travelers. Ask others for suggestions: your vet, your breeder, other dog owners, breed club members, people at the local doggie day care.

Traveling with your Field Spaniel means providing for his comfort and safety, and you will have to pack a bag for him just as you do for yourself (although you probably won't have liver treats in your own suitcase!). Bring his everyday items: food, water, bowls, leash and collar (with ID!), brush and comb, toys, bed, crate,

DOGGONE!

Wendy Ballard is the editor and publisher of the *DogGone*™ newsletter, which comes out bimonthly and features fun articles by dog owners who love to travel with their dogs. The newsletter includes information about fun places to go with your dogs, including popular vacation spots, dog-friendly hotels, parks, campgrounds, resorts, etc., as well as interesting activities to do with your dog, such as flyball, agility and much more. You can subscribe to the publication by contacting the publisher at PO Box 651155, Vero Beach, FL 32965-1155.

plus any additional accessories that he will need once you get to your vacation spot. If he takes medication, don't forget to bring it with you. If going camping or on another type of outdoor excursion, take precautions to protect your dog from ticks, mosquitoes and other pests. Above all, have a good time with your dog and enjoy each other's company!

Boarding

Today there are many options for dog owners who need someone to care for their dogs in certain circumstances. While many think of boarding their dogs as something to do when away on vacation, many others use the services of doggie "daycare" facilities, dropping their dogs off to spend the day while they are at work. Many of these facilities offer both long-term and daily care. Many go beyond just boarding and cater to all sorts of needs, with on-site grooming, veterinary care, training classes and even "web-cams" where owners can log onto the Internet and check out what their dogs are up to. Most dogs enjoy the activity and time spent with other dogs.

Before you need to use such a service, check out the ones in your area. Make visits to see the facilities, meet the staff, discuss fees and available services and see whether this is a place where you think your dog will be happy. It is best to do your research in advance so that you're not stuck at the last minute, forced into making a rushed decision without knowing whether the kennel that you've chosen meets your standards. You also can check with your vet's office to see whether they offer boarding for their clients or can recommend a good kennel in the area.

The kennel will need to see proof of your dog's health records and vaccinations so as not to spread illness from dog to dog. Your dog also will need proper identification. Owners usually experience some separation anxiety the first time they have to leave their dog in someone else's care, so it's reassuring to know that the kennel you choose is run by experienced, caring, true dog people.

You should select a suitable boarding kennel before you actually need one so that you are prepared in advance and confident about the care that your dog will receive.

TRAINING YOUR
FIELD SPANIEL

BASIC TRAINING PRINCIPLES: PUPPY VS. ADULT

There's a big difference between training an adult dog and training a young puppy. With a young puppy, everything is new! At eight to ten weeks of age, he will be experiencing many things, and he has nothing with which to compare these experiences. Up to this point, he has been with his dam and littermates, not one-on-one with people except in his interactions with his breeder and visitors to the litter.

When you first bring the puppy home, he is eager to please you. This means that he accepts doing things your way. During the next couple of months, he will absorb the basis of everything he needs to know for the rest of his life. This early age is even referred to as the "sponge" stage. After that, for the next 18 months, it's up to you to reinforce good

Incorporate commands into your daily routine so that you are continually reinforcing good behavior.

WHO'S TRAINING WHOM?

Dog training is a black-and-white exercise. The correct response to a command must be absolute, and the trainer must insist on completely accurate responses from the dog. A trainer cannot command his dog to sit and then settle for the dog's melting into the down position. Often owners are so pleased that their dogs "did something" in response to a command that they just shrug and say, "OK, down" even though they wanted the dog to sit. You want your dog to respond to the command without hesitation: he must respond at that moment and correctly every time.

manners by building on the foundation that you've established. Once your puppy is reliable in basic commands and behavior and has reached the appropriate age, you may gradually introduce him to some of the interesting sports, games and activities available to pet owners and their dogs.

Raising your puppy is a family affair. Each member of the family must know what rules to set forth for the puppy and how to use the same one-word commands to mean exactly the same thing every time. Even if yours is a large family, one person will soon be considered by the pup to be the leader, the alpha person in his pack, the "boss" who must be obeyed. Often that highly regarded person turns out to be the one who feeds the puppy. Food ranks very high on the puppy's list of important things! That's why your puppy

Even a trained adult dog should practice the basic commands on a regular basis. Fields thrive on reinforcement and praise.

is rewarded with small treats along with verbal praise when he responds to you correctly. As the puppy learns to do what you want him to do, the food rewards are gradually eliminated and only the praise remains. If you were to keep up with the food treats, you could have two problems on your hands—an obese dog and a beggar.

Training begins the minute your Field Spaniel puppy steps through the doorway of your home, so don't make the mistake of putting the puppy on the floor and telling him by your actions to "Go for it! Run wild!" Even if this is your first puppy, you must act as if you know what you're doing: be the boss. An uncertain pup may be terrified to move, while a bold one will be ready to take you at your word and start plotting to destroy the house! Before you collected your puppy, you decided where

SHOULD WE ENROLL?

If you have the means and the time, you should definitely take your dog to obedience classes. Begin with puppy kindergarten classes in which puppies of all sizes learn basic lessons while getting the opportunity to meet and greet each other; it's as much about socialization as it is about good manners. What you learn in class, you can practice at home. And if you goof up in practice, you'll get help in the next session.

The Field is an energetic and versatile dog with whom you will enjoy training and activities.

his own special place would be, and that's where to put him when you first arrive home. Give him a house tour after he has investigated his area and had a nap and a bathroom "pit stop."

It's worth mentioning here that if you've adopted an adult dog that is completely trained to your liking, lucky you! You're off the hook! However, if that dog spent his life up to this point in a kennel, or even in a good home but without any real training, be prepared to tackle the job ahead. A dog three years of age or older with no previous training cannot be blamed for not knowing what he was never taught. While the dog is trying to understand and learn your rules, at the same time he has to unlearn many of his previously self-taught habits and general view of the world.

Working with a professional trainer will speed up your progress with an adopted adult dog. You'll need patience, too. Some new rules may be close to impossible for the dog to accept. After all, he's been successful so far by doing everything his way! (Patience again.) He may agree with your instruction for a few days and then slip back into his old ways, so you must be just as consistent and understanding in your teaching as you would be with a puppy. (More patience needed yet again!) Your dog has to learn to pay attention to your voice, your family, the daily routine, new smells, new sounds and, in some cases, even a new climate.

SMILE WHEN YOU ORDER ME AROUND!

While trainers recommend practicing with your dog every day, it's perfectly acceptable to take a "mental health day" off. It's better not to train the dog on days when you're in a sour mood. Your bad attitude or lack of interest will be sensed by your dog, and he will respond accordingly. Studies show that dogs are well tuned in to their humans' emotions. Be conscious of how you use your voice when talking to your dog. Raising your voice or shouting will only erode your dog's trust in you as his trainer and master.

BE UPSTANDING!

You are the dog's leader. During training, stand up straight so your dog looks up at you, and therefore up *to* you. Say the command words distinctly, in a clear, declarative tone of voice. (No barking!) Give rewards only as the correct response takes place (remember your timing!). Praise, smiles and treats are "rewards" used to positively reinforce correct responses. Don't repeat a mistake. Just change to another exercise—you will soon find success!

One of the most important things to find out about a newly adopted adult dog is his reaction to children (yours and others), strangers and your friends, and how he acts upon meeting other dogs. If he was not socialized with dogs as a puppy, this could be a major problem. This does not mean that he's a "bad" dog, a vicious dog or an aggressive dog; rather, it means that he has no idea how to read another dog's body language. There's no way for him to tell whether the other dog is a friend or foe. Survival instinct takes over, telling him to attack first and ask questions later. This definitely calls for professional help and, even then, may not be a behavior that can be corrected 100% reliably (or even at all). If you have a puppy, this is why it is so very important to introduce your young puppy properly to other puppies and "dog-friendly" adult dogs.

HOUSE-TRAINING YOUR FIELD SPANIEL

Dogs are tactility-oriented when it comes to house-training. In other words, they respond to the surface on which they are given approval to eliminate. The choice is yours (the dog's version is in parentheses): The lawn (including the neighbors' lawns)? A bare patch of earth under a tree (where people like to sit and relax in the summertime)? Concrete steps or patio (all sidewalks, garages and basement floors)? The curbside (watch out for cars)? A small area of crushed stone in a corner of the yard (mine!)? The latter is the best choice if you can manage it, because it will remain strictly for the dog's use and is easy to keep clean.

When house-training a puppy, a key rule to live by is "what goes in must come out!"

Every puppy will welcome a snuggly place to sleep, but be sure that his bedding is washable, as "accidents" will happen.

You can start out with paper-training indoors and switch over to an outdoor surface as the puppy matures and gains control over his need to eliminate. For the nay-sayers, don't worry—this won't mean that the dog will soil on every piece of newspaper lying around the house. You are training him to go outside, remember? Starting out by paper-training often is the only choice for a city dog.

When Your Puppy's "Got to Go"

Your puppy's need to relieve himself is seemingly non-stop, but signs of improvement will be seen each week. From 8–10 weeks old, the puppy will have to be taken outside every time he wakes up, about 10–15 minutes after every meal and after every period of play—all day long, from first thing in the morning until his bedtime! That's a total of ten or more trips per day to teach the puppy where it's okay to relieve himself. With that schedule in mind, you can see that house-training a young puppy is not a part-time job. It requires someone to be home all day.

If that seems overwhelming or impossible, do a little planning. For example, plan to pick up your puppy at the start of a vacation period. If you can't get home in the middle of the day, plan to hire a dog-sitter or ask a neighbor to come over to take the pup outside, feed him his lunch and then take him out again about ten or so minutes after he's eaten. Also make arrangements with that or another person to be your "emergency" contact if you have to stay late on the job. Remind yourself—repeatedly—that this hectic schedule improves as the puppy gets older.

Home within a Home

Your Field Spaniel puppy needs to be confined to one secure, puppy-proof area when no one is able to watch his every move. Generally the kitchen is the place of choice because the floor is washable. Likewise, it's a busy family area that will accustom the pup to a variety of noises, everything from pots and pans to the telephone, blender and dishwasher. He will also be enchanted by the smell of your cooking (and will never be critical when you burn something). A sturdy exercise pen (also called an "ex-pen") can help confine a Field pup, although this is not foolproof containment as an industrious young Field will figure

Canine Development Schedule

It is important to understand how and at what age a puppy develops into adulthood. If you are a puppy owner, consult this Canine Development Schedule to determine the stage of development your puppy is currently experiencing. This knowledge will help you as you work with the puppy in the weeks and months ahead.

Period	Age	Characteristics
First to Third	Birth to Seven Weeks	Puppy needs food, sleep and warmth and responds to simple and gentle touching. Needs mother for security and disciplining. Needs littermates for learning and interacting with other dogs. Pup learns to function within a pack and learns pack order of dominance. Begin socializing pup with adults and children for short periods. Pup begins to become aware of his environment.
Fourth	Eight to Twelve Weeks	Brain is fully developed. Pup needs socializing with outside world. Remove from mother and littermates. Needs to change from canine pack to human pack. Human dominance necessary. Fear period occurs between 8 and 12 weeks. Avoid fright and pain.
Fifth	Thirteen to Sixteen Weeks	Training and formal obedience should begin. Less association with other dogs, more with people, places, situations. Period will pass easily if you remember this is pup's change-to-adolescence time. Be firm and fair. Flight instinct prominent. Permissiveness and over-disciplining can do permanent damage. Praise for good behavior.
Juvenile	Four to Eight Months	Another fear period about 7 to 8 months of age. It passes quickly, but be cautious of fright and pain. Sexual maturity reached. Dominant traits established. Dog should understand sit, down, come and stay by now.

Note: These are approximate time frames. Allow for individual differences in puppies.

out how to climb over the sides. When no one is nearby to keep tabs on him, his closed crate is the safest means of confinement. Place the pen or crate where the puppy will not get a blast of heat or air conditioning.

TIDY BOY

Clean by nature, dogs do not like to soil their dens, which in effect are their crates or sleeping quarters. Unless not feeling well, dogs will not defecate or urinate in their crates. Crate training capitalizes on the dog's natural desire to keep his den clean. Be conscientious about giving the puppy as many opportunities to relieve himself outdoors as possible. Reward the puppy for correct behavior. Praise him and pat him whenever he "goes" in the correct location. Even the tidiest of puppies can have potty accidents, so be patient and dedicate more energy to helping your puppy achieve lifelong clean habits.

If using a pen, you can put a few toys inside, along with his bed (which can be his crate if the dimensions of pen and crate are compatible) and a few layers of newspaper in one small corner, just in case. A water bowl can be hung at a convenient height on the side of the ex-pen so it won't become a splashing pool for an innovative puppy. His food dish can go on the floor, next to (but not under) the water bowl.

Crates are something that pet owners are at last getting used to for their dogs. Wild or domestic canines have always preferred to sleep in den-like safe spots, and that is exactly what the crate provides. How often have you seen adult dogs that choose to sleep under a table or chair even though they have full run of the house? It's the den connection.

In your "happy" voice, use the word "Crate" every time you put the pup into his den. If he's new to a crate, toss in a small biscuit for him to chase the first few times. At night, after he's been outside, he should sleep in his crate. The crate may be kept in his designated area at night or, if you want to be sure to hear those wake-up yips in the morning, put the crate in a corner of your bedroom. However, don't make any response whatsoever to whining or crying. If he's completely ignored, he'll settle down and get to sleep.

Good bedding for a young puppy is an old folded bath towel or an old blanket, something that is easily washable and disposable if necessary ("accidents" will happen!). Never put newspaper in the puppy's crate. Also those old ideas about adding a clock to replace his mother's heartbeat, or a hot-water bottle to replace her warmth, are just that—old ideas. The clock could drive the puppy nuts, and the hot-water bottle could end up as a very soggy waterbed! An extremely good breeder would have introduced your puppy to the crate by letting two pups sleep together for a couple of nights, followed by several nights alone. How thankful you will be if you found that breeder!

Safe toys in the pup's crate or area will keep him occupied, but monitor their condition closely. Discard any toys that show signs of being chewed to bits. Squeaky parts, bits of stuffing or plastic or any other small pieces can cause intestinal blockage or possibly choking if swallowed.

Progressing with Potty-Training

After you've taken your puppy out and he has relieved himself in the area you've selected, he can have some free time with the family as long as there is someone responsible for watching him. That doesn't mean just someone in the same room who is watching TV or busy on the computer, but one person who is doing nothing other than keeping an eye on the pup, playing with him on the floor and helping him understand his position in the pack.

This first taste of freedom will let you begin to set the house rules. If you don't want the dog on the furniture, now is the time

SOMEBODY TO BLAME

House-training a puppy can be frustrating for the puppy and the owner alike. The puppy does not instinctively understand the difference between defecating on the pavement outside and on the ceramic tile in the kitchen. He is confused and frightened by his human's exuberant reactions to his natural urges. The owner, arguably the more intelligent of the duo, is also frustrated that he cannot convince his puppy to obey his commands and instructions.

In frustration, the owner may struggle with the temptation to discipline the puppy, scold him or even strike him on the rear end. Harsh corrections are unnecessary and inappropriate, serving to defeat your purpose in gaining your puppy's trust and respect. Don't blame your nine-week-old puppy. Blame yourself for not being 100% consistent in the puppy's lessons and routine. The lesson here is simple: try harder and your puppy will succeed.

to prevent his first attempts to jump up onto the couch. The word to use in this case is "Off," not "Down." "Down" is the word you will use to teach the down position, which is something entirely different.

Most corrections at this stage come in the form of simply distracting the puppy. Instead of telling him "No" for "Don't chew the carpet," distract the chomping puppy with a toy and he'll forget about the carpet.

As you are playing with the pup, do not forget to watch him closely and pay attention to his body language. Whenever you see him begin to circle or sniff, take the puppy outside to relieve himself. If you are paper-training, put him back into his confined area on the newspapers. In either case, praise him as he eliminates while he actually is *in the act* of relieving himself. Three seconds after he has finished is too late! You'll be praising him for running toward you, picking up a toy or whatever he may be doing at that moment, and that's not what you want to be praising him for. Timing is a vital tool in all dog training. Use it!

Remove soiled newspapers immediately and replace them with clean ones. You may want to take a small piece of soiled paper and place it in the middle of the new clean papers, as the scent will attract him to that spot when it's time to go again. That scent attraction is why it's so important to clean up any messes made in the house by using a product specially made to eliminate the odor of dog urine and droppings. Regular household cleansers won't do the trick. Pet shops sell the best pet deodoriz-

DAILY SCHEDULE

How many relief trips does your puppy need per day? A puppy up to the age of 14 weeks will need to go outside about 8 to 12 times per day! You will have to take the pup out any time he starts sniffing around the floor or turning in small circles, as well as after naps, meals, games and lessons or whenever he's released from his crate. Once the puppy is 14 to 22 weeks of age, he will require only 6 to 8 relief trips. At the ages of 22 to 32 weeks, the puppy will require about 5 to 7 trips. Adult dogs typically require 4 relief trips per day, in the morning, afternoon, evening and late at night.

ers. Invest in the largest container you can find.

Scent attraction eventually will lead your pup to his chosen spot outdoors; this is the basis of outdoor training. When you take your puppy outside to relieve himself, use a one-word command such as "Outside" or "Go-potty" (that's one word to the puppy!) as you pick him up and attach his leash. Then put him down in his area. If he is too big for you to carry, snap the leash on quickly and lead him to his spot. Now comes the hard part—hard for you, that is. Just stand there until he urinates and defecates. Move him a few feet in one direction or another if he's just sitting there looking at you, but remember that this is neither playtime nor time for a walk. This is strictly a business trip! Then, as he circles and squats (remember your timing!), give him a quiet "Good dog" as praise. If you start to jump for joy, ecstatic over his performance, he'll do one of two things: either he will stop mid-stream, as it were, or he'll do it again for you—in the house—and expect you to be just as delighted!

Give him five minutes or so and, if he doesn't go in that time, take him back indoors to his confined area and try again in another ten minutes, or immediately if you see him sniffing and circling. By careful observation, you'll soon work out a successful schedule.

Accidents, by the way, are just that—accidents. Clean them up quickly and thoroughly, without comment, after the puppy has been taken outside to finish his business and then put back into his area or crate. If you witness an accident in progress, say "No!" in a stern voice and get the pup outdoors immedi-

Most breeders concur that males, more fixed on their toileting habits, require more patience to house-train than do females.

LEADER OF THE PACK

Canines are pack animals. They live according to pack rules, and every pack has only one leader. Guess what? That's you! To establish your position of authority, lay down the rules and be fair and good-natured in all your dealings with your dog. He will consider young children as his littermates, but the one who trains him, who feeds him, who grooms him, who expects him to come into line, that's his leader. And he who leads must be obeyed.

Fields require daily physical activity, including games and obedience practice to engage the body and mind.

ately. No punishment is needed. You and your puppy are just learning each other's language, and sometimes it's easy to miss a puppy's message. Chalk it up to experience and watch more closely from now on.

KEEPING THE PACK ORDERLY

Discipline is a form of training that brings order to life. For example, military discipline is what allows the soldiers in an army to work as one. Discipline is a form of teaching and, in dogs, is the basis of how the successful pack operates. Each member knows his place in the pack and all respect the leader, or alpha dog. It is essential for your puppy that you establish this type of relationship, with you as the alpha, or leader. It is a form of social coexistence that all canines recognize and accept. Discipline, therefore, is never to be confused with punishment. When you teach your puppy how you want him to behave, and he behaves properly and you praise him for it, you are disciplining him with a form of positive reinforcement.

For a dog, rewards come in the form of praise, a smile, a cheerful tone of voice, a few friendly pats or a rub of the ears. Rewards are also small food treats. Obviously, that does not mean bits of regular dog food. Instead, treats are very small bits of special things like cheese or pieces of soft dog treats. The idea is to reward the dog with something very small that he can taste and swallow, providing instant positive reinforcement. If he has to take time to chew the treat, he will have forgotten what he did to earn it by the time he is finished!

Your puppy should never be physically punished. The displeasure shown on your face and in your voice is sufficient to signal to the pup that he has done something wrong. He wants to please everyone higher up on the social ladder, especially his leader, so a

TEACHER'S PET

Dogs are individuals, not robots, with many traits basic to their breed. Some, bred to work alone, are independent thinkers; others rely on you to call the shots. If you have enrolled in a training class, your instructor can offer alternative methods of training based on your individual dog's instincts and personality. You may benefit from using a different type of collar or switching to a class with different kinds of dogs.

KEEP IT SIMPLE—AND FUN
Keep your lessons simple, interesting and user-friendly. Fun breaks help you both. Spend two minutes or ten teaching your puppy, but practice only as long as your dog enjoys what he's doing and is focused on pleasing you. If he's bored or distracted, stop the training session after any correct response (always end on a high note!). After a few minutes of playtime, you can go back to "hitting the books."

scowl and harsh voice will take care of the error. Growling out the word "Shame!" when the pup is caught in the act of doing something wrong is better than the repetitive "No." Some dogs hear "No" so often that they begin to think it's their name! By the way, do not use the dog's name when you're correcting him. His name is reserved to get his attention for something pleasant about to take place.

There are punishments that have nothing to do with you. For example, your dog may think that chasing cats is one reason for his existence. You can try to stop it as much as you like but without success, because it's such fun for the dog. But one good hissing, spitting swipe of a cat's claws across the dog's nose will put an end to the game forever. Intervene only when your dog's eyeball is seriously at risk. Cat scratches can cause permanent damage to an innocent but annoying puppy.

PUPPY KINDERGARTEN

COLLAR AND LEASH

Before you begin your Field Spaniel puppy's education, he must be used to his collar and leash. Choose a collar for your puppy that is secure, but not heavy or bulky. He won't enjoy training if he's uncomfortable. A flat buckle collar is fine for everyday wear and for initial puppy training. For older dogs, there are several types of training collars such as the martingale, which is a double loop that tightens slightly around the neck, or the head collar, which is similar to a horse's halter. Before using any type of training collar, ask for advice from your breeder or

Dogs learn to respond to verbal commands and body language. Advanced activities and competition can require a dog to complete exercises based on hand signals only.

a trainer regarding what type of collar is best for the breed. With any type of training collar, you must learn how to put it on your dog properly and the correct way to use it.

BASIC PRINCIPLES OF DOG TRAINING

1. Start training early. A young puppy is ready, willing and able.
2. Timing is your all-important tool. Praise at the exact time that the dog responds correctly. Pay close attention.
3. Patience is almost as important as timing!
4. Repeat! The same word has to mean the same thing every time.
5. In the beginning, praise all correct behavior verbally, along with treats and petting.

A lightweight 6-foot woven cotton or nylon training leash is preferred by most trainers because it is easy to fold up in your hand and comfortable to hold because there is a certain amount of give to it. There are lessons where the dog will start off 6 feet away from you at the end of the leash. The leash used to take the puppy outside to relieve himself is shorter because you don't want him to roam away from his area. The shorter leash will also be the one to use when you walk the puppy.

If you've been wise enough to enroll in a puppy kindergarten training class, suggestions will be made as to the best collar and leash for your young puppy. I say "wise" because your puppy will be in a class with puppies in his age range (up to five months old) of all breeds and sizes. It's the perfect way for him to learn the right way (and the wrong way) to interact with other dogs as well as their people. You cannot teach your puppy how to interpret another dog's sign language. For a first-time puppy owner, these socialization classes are invaluable. For experienced dog owners, they are a real boon to further training.

ATTENTION

You've been using the dog's name since the minute you collected him from the breeder, so you should be able to get his attention by saying his name—with a big smile and in an excited tone of voice. His response will be the puppy equivalent of "Here I am! What are we going to do?" Your immediate response (if you haven't guessed by now) is "Good dog." Rewarding him at the moment he pays attention to you teaches him the proper way to respond when he hears his name.

EXERCISES FOR A BASIC CANINE EDUCATION

The Sit Exercise

There are several ways to teach the puppy to sit. The first one is to catch him whenever he is about to sit and, as his backside nears the floor, say "Sit, good dog!" That's positive reinforcement and, if your timing is sharp, he will learn that what he's doing at that second is connected to your saying "Sit" and that you think he's clever for doing it!

Another method is to start with the puppy on his leash in front of you. Show him a treat in the palm of your right hand. Bring your hand up under his nose and, almost in slow motion, move your hand up and back so his nose goes up in the air and his head tilts back as he follows the treat in your hand. At that point, he will have to either sit or fall over, so as his back legs buckle under, say "Sit, good dog," and then give him the treat and lots of praise. You may have to begin with your hand lightly running up his chest, actually lifting his chin up until he sits. Some (usually older) dogs require gentle pressure on their hindquarters with the left hand, in which case the dog should be on your left side. Puppies generally do not appreciate this physical dominance.

The sit forms the basis of other exercises, such as the sit/stay, shown here. This Field is intently focused on the lesson at hand.

After a few times, you should be able to show the dog a treat in the open palm of your hand, raise your hand waist-high as you say "Sit" and have him sit. Thereby, you are teaching him two things at the same time. Both the verbal

Gentle guidance may be needed when showing your Field the proper sit position.

command and the motion of the hand are signals for the sit. Your puppy is watching you almost more than he is listening to you, so what you do is just as important as what you say.

Don't save any of these drills only for training sessions. Use them as much as possible at odd times during a normal day. The dog should always sit before being given his food dish. He should sit to let you go through a doorway first, when the doorbell rings or when you stop to speak to someone on the street.

The Down Exercise

Before beginning to teach the down command, you must consider how the dog feels about this exercise. To him, "down" is a submissive position. Being flat on the floor with you standing over him is not his idea of fun. It's up to you to let him know that, while it may not be fun, the reward of your approval is worth his effort.

Start with the puppy on your left side in a sit position. Hold the leash right above his collar in your left hand. Have an extra-special treat, such as a small piece of cooked chicken or hot dog, in your right hand. Place it at the end of the pup's nose and steadily move your hand down and forward along the ground. Hold the leash to prevent a sudden lunge for the food. As the puppy goes into the down position, say "Down" very gently.

The difficulty with this exercise is twofold: it's both the submissive aspect and the fact that most people say the word "Down" as if they were drill sergeants in charge of recruits! So issue the command sweetly, give him the treat and have the pup maintain the down position for

SIT AROUND THE HOUSE

"Sit" is the command you'll use most often. Your pup objects when placed in a sit with your hands, so try the "bringing the food up under his chin" method. Better still, catch him in the act! Your dog will sit on his own many times throughout the day, so let him know that he's doing the "Sit" by rewarding him. Praise him and have him sit for everything—toys, connecting his leash, his dinner, before going out the door, etc.

DOWN

"Down" is a harsh-sounding word and a submissive posture in dog body language, thus presenting two obstacles in teaching the down command. When the dog is about to flop down on his own, tell him "Good down." Pups that are not good about being handled learn better by having food lowered in front of them. A dog that trusts you can be gently guided into position. When you give the command "Down," be sure to say it sweetly!

several seconds. If he tries to get up immediately, place your hands on his shoulders and press down gently, giving him a very quiet "Good dog." As you progress with this lesson, increase the "down time" until he will hold it until you say "Okay" (his cue for release). Practice this one in the house at various times throughout the day.

By increasing the length of time during which the dog must maintain the down position, you'll find many uses for it. For example, he can lie at your feet in the vet's office or anywhere that both of you have to wait, when you are on the phone, while the family is eating and so forth. If you progress to training for competitive obedience, he'll already be all set for the exercise called the "long down."

The Stay Exercise

You can teach your Field Spaniel to stay in the sit, down and stand positions. To teach the sit/stay, have the dog sit on your left side. Hold the leash at waist level in your left hand and let the dog know that you have a treat in your closed right hand. Step forward on your right foot as you say "Stay." Immediately turn and stand directly in front of the dog, keeping your right hand up high so he'll keep his eye on the treat hand and maintain the sit position for a count of five. Return to your original position and offer the reward.

Increase the length of the sit/stay each time until the dog can hold it for at least 30 seconds without moving. After about a week of success, move out on your right foot and take two steps before turn-

A show dog must be well versed in the basics. This handsome Field stays in a standing position, which is the required pose for the judge's evaluation.

The down/stay is taught once the dog is comfortable and confident with the down exercise.

ing to face the dog. Give the "Stay" hand signal (left palm held up, facing the dog) as you leave. He gets the treat when you return and he holds the sit/stay. Increase the distance that you walk away from him before turning until you reach the length of your training leash. But don't rush it! Go back to the beginning if he moves before he should. No matter what the lesson, never be upset by having to back up for a few days. The repetition and practice are what will make your dog reliable in these commands. It won't do any good to move on to something more difficult if the command is not mastered at the easier levels. Above all, even if you do get frustrated, never let your puppy know! Always keep a positive, upbeat attitude during training, which will transmit to your dog for positive results.

The down/stay is taught in the same way once the dog is completely reliable and steady with the down command. Again, don't rush it. With the dog in the down position on your left side, step out on your right foot as you say "Stay." Return by walking around in back of the dog and into your original position. While you are training, it's okay to murmur something like "Hold on" to encourage him to stay put. When the dog will stay without moving when you are at a distance of 3 or

TIPS FOR TRAINING AND SAFETY

1. Whether on or off leash, practice only in a fenced area.
2. Remove the training collar when the training session is over.
3. Don't try to break up a dogfight.
4. "Come," "Leave it" and "Wait" are safety commands.
5. The dog belongs in a crate or behind a barrier when riding in the car.
6. Don't ignore the dog's first sign of aggression. Aggression only gets worse, so take it seriously.
7. Keep the faces of children and dogs separated.
8. Pay attention to what the dog is chewing.
9. Keep the vet's number near your phone.
10. "Okay" is a useful release command.

TIME TO PLAY!

Playtime can happen both indoors and out. A young puppy is growing so rapidly that he needs sleep more than he needs a lot of physical exercise. Puppies get sufficient exercise on their own just through normal puppy activity. Monitor play with young children so you can remove the puppy when he's had enough, or calm the kids if they get too rowdy. Almost all puppies love to chase after a toy you've thrown, and you can turn your games into educational activities. Every time your puppy brings the toy back to you, say "Give it" (or "Drop it") followed by "Good dog" and throwing it again. If he's reluctant to give it to you, offer a small treat so that he drops the toy as he takes the treat. He will soon get the idea.

4 feet, begin to increase the length of time before you return. Be sure he holds the down on your return until you say "Okay." At that point, he gets his treat—just so he'll remember for next time that it's not over until it's over.

The Come Exercise

No command is more important to the safety of your Field Spaniel than "Come." It is what you should say every single time you see the puppy running toward you: "Binky, come! Good dog." During playtime, run a few feet away from the puppy and turn and tell him to "Come" as he is already running to you. You can go so far as to teach your puppy two things at once if you squat down and hold out your arms. As the pup gets close to you and you're saying "Good dog," bring your right arm in about waist high. Now he's also learning the hand signal, an excellent device should you be on the phone when you need to get him to come to you! You'll also both be one step ahead when you enter obedience classes.

When the puppy responds to your well-timed "Come," try it with the puppy on the training leash. This time, catch him off guard, while he's sniffing a leaf or watching a bird: "Binky, come!" You may have to pause for a split second after his name to be sure you have his attention. If the puppy shows any sign of confusion, give the leash a mild jerk and take a couple of steps backward. Do not repeat the command. In this case, you should say "Good come" as he reaches you.

Make it fun! The Field's natural retrieving abilities can be used in teaching the dog to come when called.

You can progress to formal retrieve training once your Field responds reliably to the basic commands.

That's the number-one rule of training. Each command word is given just once. Anything more is nagging. You'll also notice that all commands are one word only. Even when they are actually two words, you say them as one.

Never call the dog to come to you—with or without his name—if you are angry or intend to correct him for some misbehavior. When correcting the pup, you go to him. Your dog must always connect "Come" with something pleasant and with your approval; then you can rely on his response.

Puppies, like children, have notoriously short attention spans, so don't overdo it with any of the training. Keep each lesson short. Break it up with a quick run around the yard or a ball toss, repeat the lesson and quit as soon as the pup gets it right. That way, you will always end with a "Good dog."

Life isn't perfect and neither are puppies. A time will come, often around ten months of age, when he'll become "selectively deaf" or choose to "forget" his name. He may respond by wagging his tail (and even seeming to smile at you) with a look that says "Make me!" Laugh, throw his favorite toy and skip the lesson you had planned. Pups will be pups!

The Heel Exercise

The second most important command to teach, after the come, is the heel. When you are walking your growing puppy, you need to be in control. Besides, it looks terrible to be pulled and yanked down the street, and it's not much fun either. Your eight- to ten-week-old puppy will probably follow you everywhere, but that's his natural instinct, not your control over the situation.

RELIABLE RECALL

It is essential for a puppy to be taught a reliable recall command (come). Field Spaniels not taught at an early age that coming when called is essential may become runners. It is for the good of the dog that a reliable recall is a must; a dog that does not reliably come when called cannot be called out of danger.

However, any time he does follow you, you can say "Heel" and be ahead of the game, as he will learn to associate this command with the action of following you before you even begin teaching him to heel.

There is a very precise, almost military, procedure for teaching your dog to heel. As with all other obedience training, begin with the dog on your left side. He will be in a very nice sit and you will have the training leash across your chest. Hold the loop and folded leash in your right hand. Pick up the slack leash above the dog in your left hand and hold it loosely at your side. Step out on your left foot as you say "Heel." If the puppy does not move, give a gentle tug or pat your left leg to get him started. If he surges ahead of you, stop and pull him back gently until he is at your side. Tell him to sit and begin again.

Walk a few steps and stop while the puppy is correctly beside you. Tell him to sit and give mild verbal praise. (More enthusiastic praise will encourage him to think the lesson is over.) Repeat the lesson, increasing the number of steps you take only as long as the dog is heeling nicely beside you. When you end the lesson, have him hold the sit, then give him the "Okay" to let him know that this is the end of the lesson. Praise him so that he knows he did a good job.

The cure for excessive pulling (a common problem) is to stop when the dog is no more than 2 or 3 feet ahead of you. Guide him back into position and begin again. With a really determined puller, try switching to a head collar. This will automatically turn the pup's head toward you so you can bring him back easily to the heel position. Give quiet, reassuring praise

LET'S GO!

Many people use "Let's go" instead of "Heel" when teaching their dogs to behave on lead. It sounds more like fun! When beginning to teach the heel, whatever command you use, always step off on your left foot. That's the one next to the dog, who is on your left side, in case you've forgotten. Keep a loose leash. When the dog pulls ahead, stop, bring him back and begin again. Use treats to guide him around turns.

every time the leash goes slack and he's staying with you.

Staying and heeling can take a lot out of a dog, so provide playtime and free-running exercise to shake off the stress when the lessons are over. You don't want him to associate training with all work and no fun.

NO MORE TREATS!

When your dog is responding promptly and correctly to commands, it's time to eliminate treats. Begin by alternating a treat reward with a verbal-praise-only reward. Gradually eliminate all treats while increasing the frequency of praise. Overlook pleading eyes and expectant expressions, but if he's still watching your treat hand, you're on your way to using hand signals.

OBEDIENCE CLASSES

The advantages of an obedience class are that your dog will have to learn amid the distractions of other people and dogs and that your mistakes will be quickly corrected by the trainer. Teaching your dog along with a qualified instructor and other handlers who may have more dog experience than you is another plus of the class environment. The instructor and other handlers can help you to find the most efficient way of teaching your dog a command or exercise. It's often easier to learn by other people's mistakes than your own. You will also learn all of the requirements for competitive obedience trials, in which you can earn titles and go on to advanced jumping and retrieving exercises, which are fun for many dogs. Obedience classes build the foundation needed for many other canine activities (in which we humans are allowed to participate, too!).

TRAINING FOR OTHER ACTIVITIES

Whether a dog is trained in the structured environment of a class or alone with his owner at home, there are many activities that can bring fun and rewards to both owner and dog once they have mastered basic control. Field Spaniels love to be involved with their owners, and activities abound in which you and your Field may enjoy each other's company in learning new skills.

Teaching the dog to help out around the home, in the yard or on the farm provides great satisfaction to both dog and owner. In addition, the dog's help makes life a little easier for his owner and raises his stature as a valued companion to his family. It helps give the dog a purpose by occupying his mind and providing an outlet for his energy. For those who like to volunteer, there is the

If you have any intention of showing your Field Spaniel, be ready to commit to training and preparing for the ring. Judges appreciate a professional performance from dog and handler.

wonderful feeling of owning a therapy dog and visiting hospices, nursing homes and veterans' homes to bring smiles, comfort and companionship to those who live there.

If you are interested in participating in organized activities or competition with your Field Spaniel, there is a variety of pursuits in which you and your dog can become involved.

HUNTING

As a gundog, Field Spaniels are well suited for hunting game appropriate to their size. They are often used to locate and flush upland game birds, later retrieving the shot game to their handlers back from land or water. Fanciers have also reported success in using Field Spaniels on rabbit. They are typically tenacious and thorough in working cover. For those who do not hunt but who wish to develop the Field Spaniel's natural abilities, consider competitive hunting events.

CONFORMATION AND JUNIOR SHOWMANSHIP

There are many Field Spaniel devotees who purchased their first Fields strictly for companionship, only to find that, when visiting dog shows and meeting other Field Spaniel owners and handlers, they were attracted to dog-show competition themselves! Conformation competition is where the prized title of Champion can be earned. The American Kennel Club promotes involvement of youngsters in dog handling through its Junior Showmanship program, truly making showing a family affair. Many local kennel clubs offer classes where aspiring exhibitors of any age can learn the skills they will need in the show ring.

TRACKING

Field Spaniels excel in tracking. The large nose of the Field Spaniel is ideally suited and able to work in a variety of situations that capitalize on the breed's purposeful and powerful scenting ability. Field Spaniels have been trained to use their noses in search-and-rescue work, narcotics detection and other similar endeavors in addition to training for participation in tracking tests. The AKC offers a tracking program and there are many clubs throughout the US that hold their own tracking events and offer training.

ASSISTANCE AND THERAPY WORK

A number of Field Spaniels actively participate as therapy dogs, ranging from specially trained dogs who visit nursing homes and other group-care facilities to dogs who actively provide assistance. In functioning as an assistance dog, regard must be given to the overall size of the

Field Spaniel. For example, a Field Spaniel is not going to make a suitable guide dog for the blind due to his more compact size, but he does well as a hearing dog. The breed's natural affinity for humans, desire to please and problem-solving ability make Fields well suited to this sort of training.

Obedience, Agility and Rally

A trained Field Spaniel is a joy to live with. Training and activity provide appropriate outlets for the breed's considerable ability to learn and solve problems, and the Field Spaniel loves doing things with his owners! It is a common recommendation that all Field Spaniel puppies be taken through a basic companion obedience class at the minimum, as the skills learned are valuable for a lifetime and also serve as the foundation for more advanced training and competition if the owner desires. The American Kennel Club offers both obedience and agility titling programs, and there are dog clubs across the country that offer training and practice courses.

A recent addition to the world of competitive canine sports is known as "rally obedience." This event is somewhat of a combination of obedience and agility and has been met with huge popularity. Rally obedience is still new, but Field Spaniels have been among the first to try out this new venue of competition.

Your Field is a fun and personable companion with a sparkling sense of humor and a talent for all types of antics.

Be aware that agility, advanced obedience and rally training require a dog to perform different types of jumps. Care must be taken to avoid stress on a dog's developing skeletal structure. Jump training and other strenuous training must begin only once a young dog has reached an appropriate age. Jumping must be taught systematically and with care to assure good form and prevent avoidable injury. Begin with very low jump heights and progress to higher heights slowly. Seek out a local training group who can advise you about how to teach your Field Spaniel these skills properly and safely.

Physical Structure of the Field Spaniel

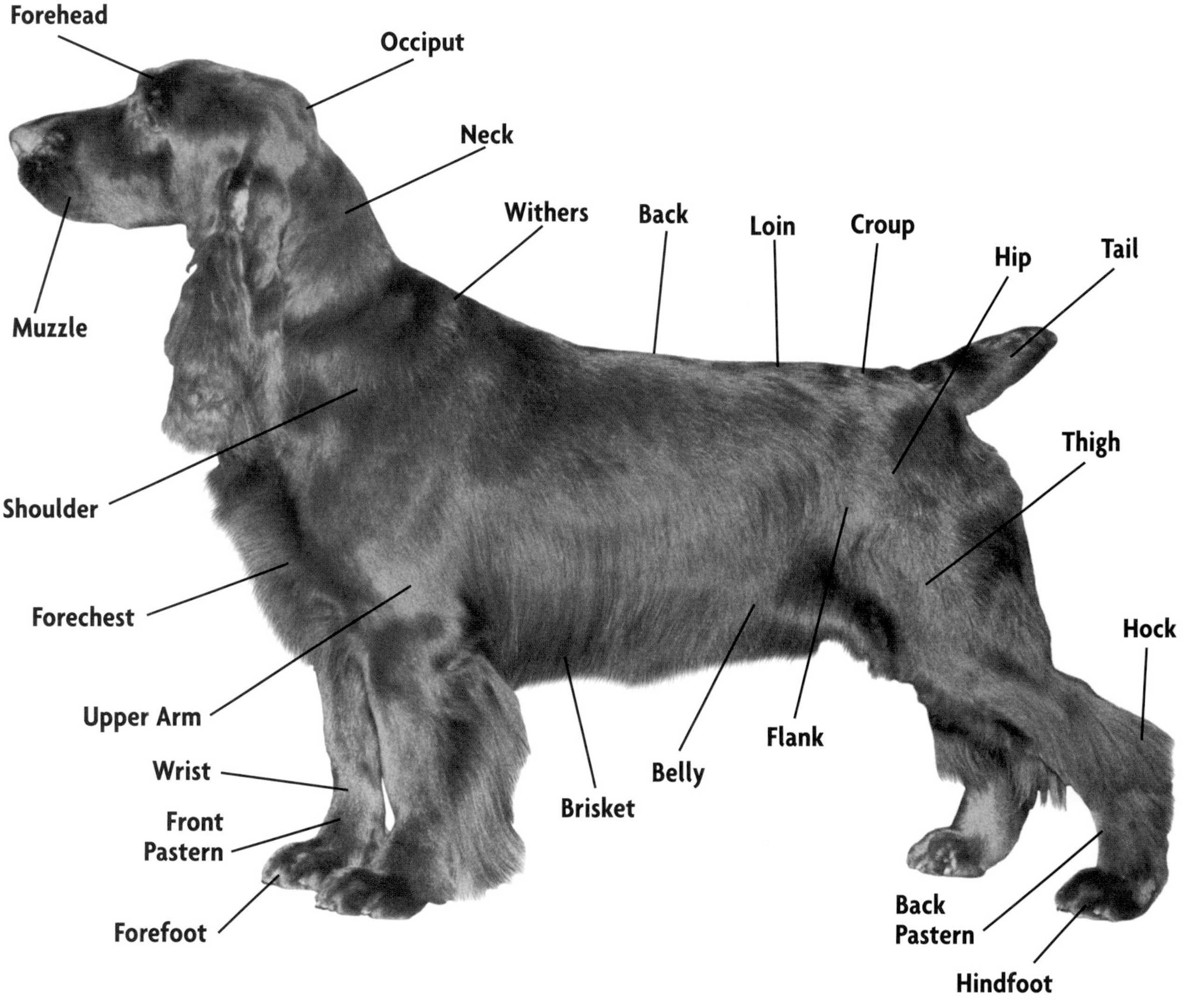

HEALTHCARE OF YOUR
FIELD SPANIEL

BY LOWELL ACKERMAN DVM, DACVD

HEALTHCARE FOR A LIFETIME

When you own a dog, you become his healthcare advocate over his entire lifespan, as well as being the one to shoulder the financial burden of such care. Accordingly, it is worthwhile to focus on prevention rather than treatment, as you and your pet will both be happier.

Of course, the best place to have begun your program of preventive healthcare is with the initial purchase or adoption of your dog. There is no way of guaranteeing that your new furry friend is free of medical problems, but there are some things you can do to improve your odds. You certainly should have done adequate research into the Field Spaniel and have selected your puppy carefully rather than buying on impulse. Health issues aside, a large number of pet abandonment and relinquishment cases arise from a mismatch between pet needs and owner expectations. This is entirely preventable with appropriate planning and finding a good breeder.

Regarding healthcare issues specifically, it is very difficult to make blanket statements about where to acquire a problem-free pet, but, again, a reputable breeder is your best bet. In an ideal situation you have the opportunity to see both parents, get references from other owners of the breeder's pups and see genetic-testing documentation for several generations of the litter's ancestors. At the very least, you must thoroughly investigate the Field Spaniel and the problems inherent in that breed, as well as the genetic testing available to screen for those problems. Genetic testing offers some important benefits but is available for only a few disorders in a relatively small number of breeds and is not available for some of the most common genetic diseases, such as hip dysplasia, cataracts, epilepsy, cardiomyopathy, etc. This area of research is indeed exciting and increasingly important, and advances will continue to be made each year. In fact, recent research has shown that there is an equivalent dog gene for 75% of known human genes, so research done in either species is likely to benefit the other.

We've also discussed that evaluating the behavioral nature of

INTERNAL ORGANS OF THE FIELD SPANIEL

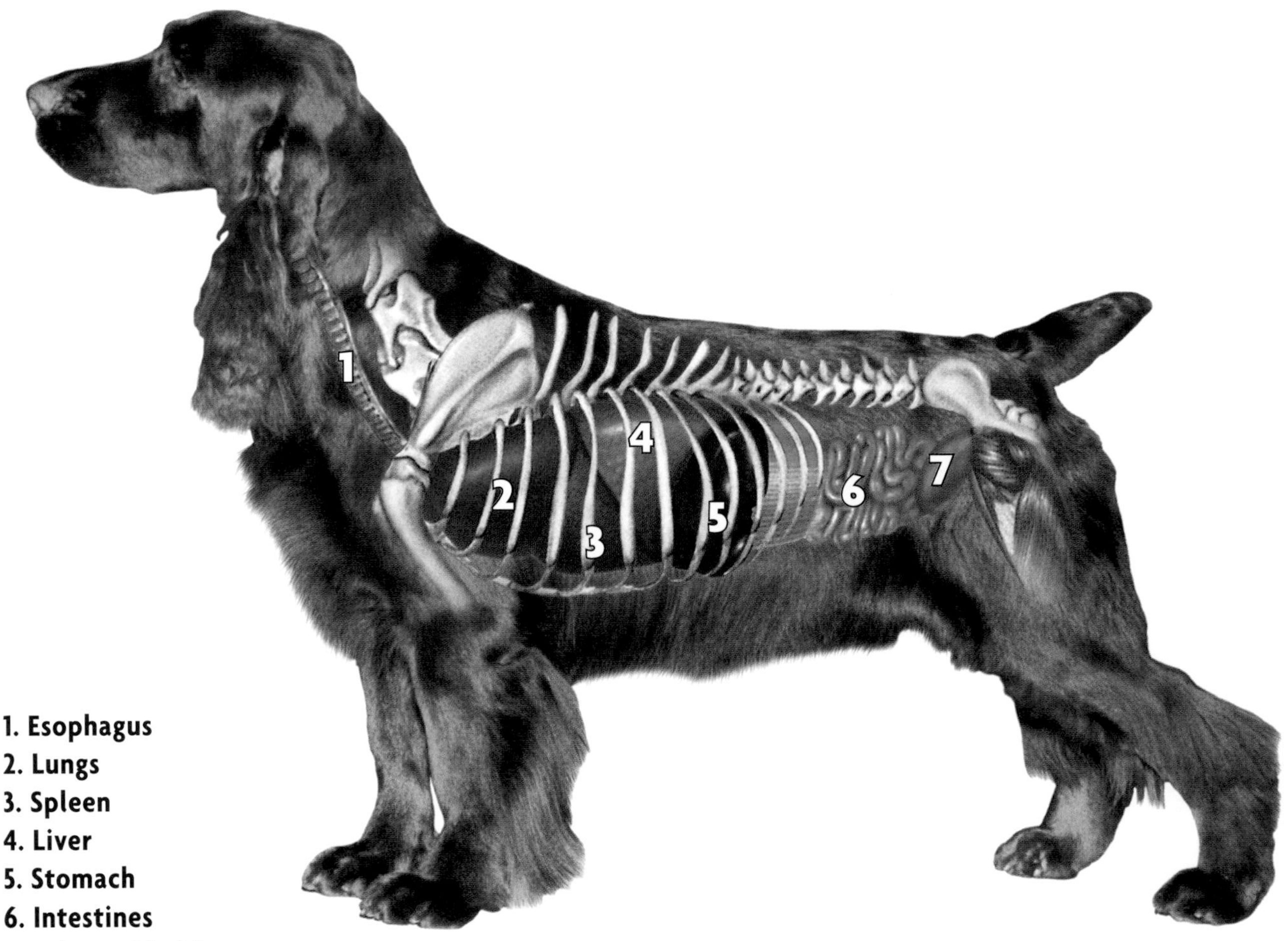

1. Esophagus
2. Lungs
3. Spleen
4. Liver
5. Stomach
6. Intestines
7. Urinary Bladder

your Field Spaniel and that of his immediate family members is an important part of the selection process that cannot be underestimated or overemphasized. It is sometimes difficult to evaluate temperament in puppies because certain behavioral tendencies, such as some forms of aggression, may not be immediately evident. More dogs are euthanized each year for behavioral reasons than for all medical conditions combined, so it is critical to take temperament issues seriously. Start with a well-balanced, friendly companion and put the time and effort into proper socialization, and you will both be rewarded with a valued relationship for the life of the dog.

Assuming that you have started off with a pup from healthy, sound stock, you then become responsible for helping your veterinarian keep your pet healthy. Some crucial things happen before you even bring your puppy home. Parasite control typically begins at two weeks of age, and vaccinations typically begin at six to eight weeks of age. A pre-pubertal evaluation is typically scheduled for about six months of age. At this time, a dental evaluation is done (since the adult teeth are now in), heartworm prevention is started and neutering or spaying is most commonly done.

It is critical to commence regular dental care at home if you have not already done so. It may not sound very important, but most dogs have active periodontal disease by four years of age if they don't have their teeth cleaned regularly at home, not just at their veterinary exams. Dental problems lead to more than just bad "doggy breath." Gum disease can have very serious medical consequences. If you start brushing

DENTAL WARNING SIGNS

A veterinary dental exam is necessary if you notice one or any combination of the following in your dog:

- Broken, loose or missing teeth
- Loss of appetite (which could be due to mouth pain or illness caused by infection)
- Gum abnormalities, including redness, swelling and bleeding
- Drooling, with or without blood
- Yellowing of the teeth or gumline, indicating tartar
- Bad breath

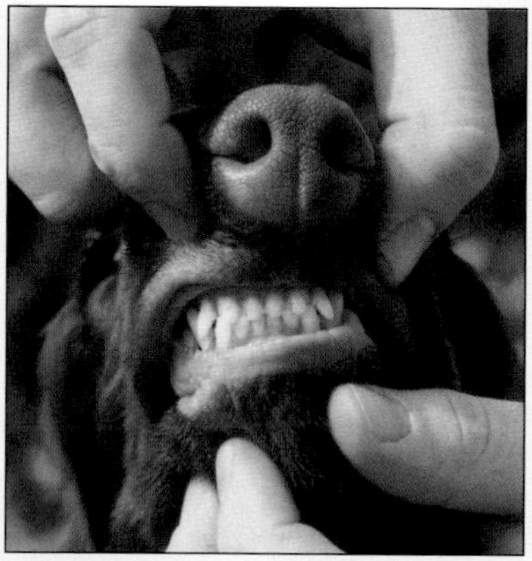

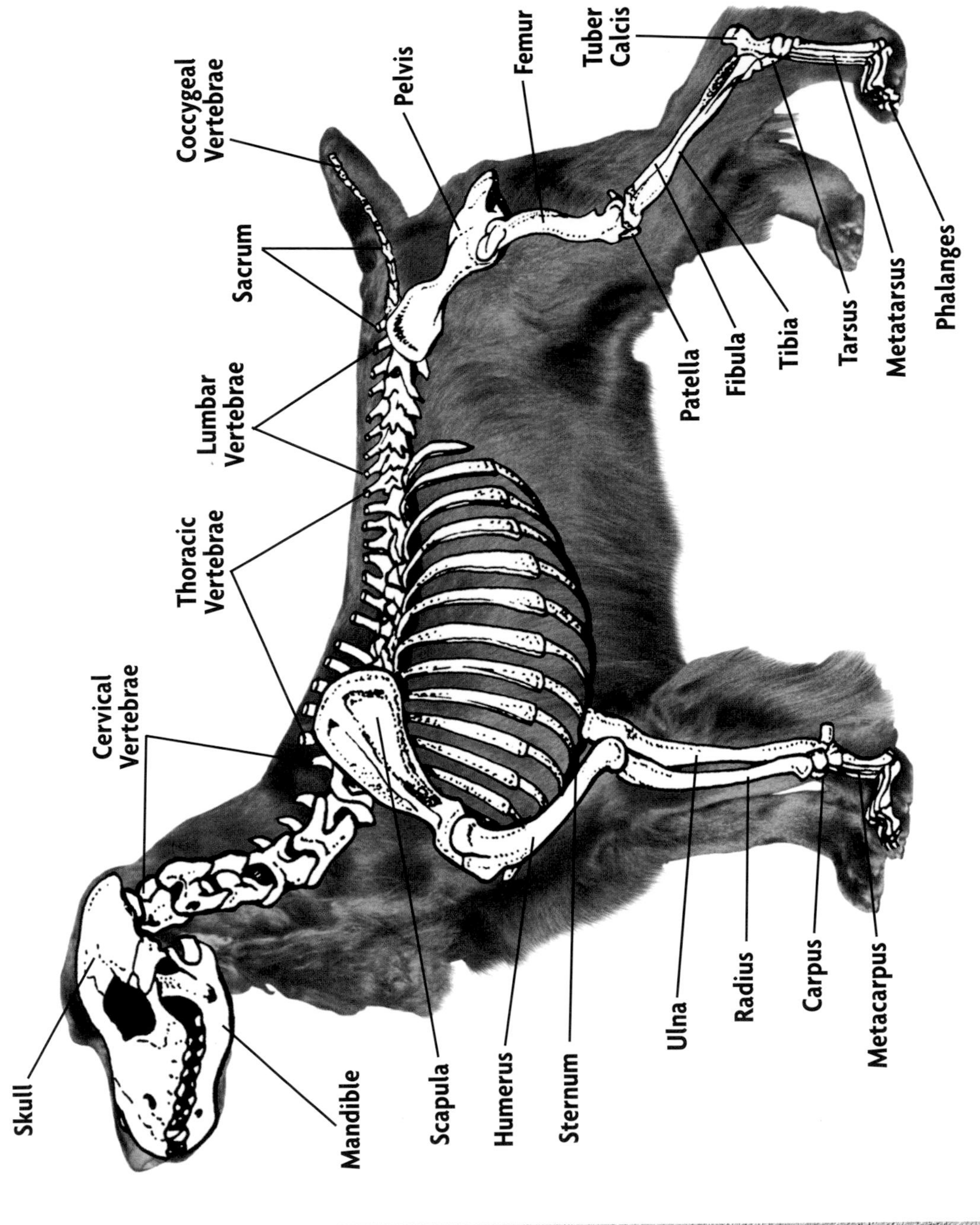

SKELETAL STRUCTURE OF THE FIELD SPANIEL

your dog's teeth and using antiseptic rinses from a young age, your dog will be accustomed to it and will not resist. The results will be healthy dentition, which your pet will need to enjoy a long, healthy life.

Most dogs are considered adults at a year of age, although Field Spaniels are not fully mature until about three years of age. Even individual dogs within each breed have different healthcare requirements, so work with your veterinarian to determine what will be needed and what your role should be. This doctor-client relationship is important, because as vaccination guidelines change, there may not be an annual "vaccine visit" scheduled. You must make sure that you see your veterinarian at least annually, even if no vaccines are due, because this is the best opportunity to coordinate healthcare activities and to make sure that no medical issues creep by unaddressed.

As your Field Spaniel reaches his senior years, he will start to require some special care. In general, if you've been taking great care of your canine companion throughout his formative and adult years, the transition to senior status should be a smooth one. Age is not a disease, and as long as everything is functioning as it should, there is no reason why most of late adulthood should not be rewarding for both you and your pet. This is especially true if you have tended to the details, such as regular veterinary visits, proper dental care, excellent nutrition and management of bone and joint issues.

HIT ME WITH A HOT SPOT

What is a hot spot? Technically known as pyotraumatic dermatitis, a hot spot is an infection on the dog's coat, usually by the rear end, under the tail or on a leg, which the dog inflicts upon himself. The dog licks and bites the itchy spot until it becomes inflamed and infected. The hot spot can range in size from the circumference of a grape to the circumference of an apple. Provided that the hot spot is not related to a deeper bacterial infection, it can be treated topically by clipping the area, cleaning the sore and giving prednisone. For bacterial infections, antibiotics are required. In some cases, an Elizabethan collar is required to keep the dog from further irritating the hot spot. The itching can intensify and the pain becomes worse. Medicated shampoos and cool compresses, drying agents and topical steroids may be prescribed by your vet as well.

Hot spots can be caused by fleas, an allergy, an ear infection, anal sac problems, mange or a foreign irritant. Likewise, they can be linked to psychoses. The underlying problem must be addressed in addition to the hot spot itself.

At this stage in your Field Spaniel's life, your veterinarian will want to schedule visits twice yearly, instead of once, to run some laboratory screenings, electrocardiograms and the like, and to change the diet to something more digestible. Catching problems early is the best way to manage them effectively. Treating the early stages of heart disease is so much easier than trying to intervene when there is more significant damage to the heart muscle. Similarly, managing the beginning of kidney problems is fairly routine if there is no significant kidney damage. Other problems, like cognitive dysfunction (similar to senility and Alzheimer's disease), cancer, diabetes and arthritis, are more common in older dogs, but all can be treated to help the dog live as many happy, comfortable years as possible. Just as in people, medical management is more effective (and less expensive) when you catch things early.

SELECTING A VETERINARIAN

There is probably no more important decision that you will make regarding your pet's healthcare than the selection of his doctor. Your pet's veterinarian will be a pediatrician, family-practice physician and gerontologist, depending on the dog's life stage, and will be the individual who makes recommendations regarding issues such as when specialists need to be consulted, when diagnostic testing and/or therapeutic intervention is needed and when you will need to seek outside emergency and critical-care services. Your vet will act as your advocate and liaison throughout these processes.

Everyone has his own idea about what to look for in a vet, an individual who will play a big role in his dog's (and, of course, his own) life for many years to come. For some, it is the compassionate caregiver with whom they hope to develop a professional relationship to span the lives of their dogs and even their future pets. For others, they are seeking a clinician with keen diagnostic and therapeutic insight who can deliver state-of-the-art healthcare. Still others need a veterinary facility that is open evenings and weekends, is in close proximity or provides mobile veterinary services to accommodate their schedules; these people may not much mind that their dogs might see different veterinarians on each visit. Just as we have different reasons for selecting our own healthcare professionals (e.g., covered by insurance plan, expert in field, convenient location, etc.), we should not expect that there is a one-size-fits-all recommendation for selecting a veterinarian and veterinary practice. The best advice is to be honest in your assessment of what you expect from a veterinary practice and to conscientiously research the options in your area. You will quickly appreciate that not all veterinary practices are the same, and you will be happiest with one that truly meets your needs.

There is another point to be considered in the selection of veterinary services. Not that long ago, a single veterinarian would attempt to manage all medical and surgical issues as they arose. That was often problematic, because veterinarians are trained in many species and many diseases, and it was just impossible for general veterinary practitioners to be experts in every species, every breed, every field and every ailment. However, just as in the human healthcare fields, specialization has allowed general practitioners to concentrate on primary healthcare delivery, especially wellness and the prevention of infectious diseases, and to utilize a network of specialists to assist in the management of conditions that require specific expertise and experience. Thus there are now many types of veterinary specialists, including dermatologists, cardiologists, ophthalmologists, surgeons, internists, oncologists, neurologists, behaviorists, criticalists and others to help primary-care veterinarians deal

YOUR DOG NEEDS TO VISIT THE VET IF:

- He has ingested a toxin such as antifreeze or a toxic plant; in these cases, administer first aid and call the vet right away
- His teeth are discolored, loose or missing or he has sores or other signs of infection or abnormality in the mouth
- He has been vomiting, has had diarrhea or has been constipated for over 24 hours; call immediately if you notice blood
- He has refused food for over 24 hours
- His eating habits, water intake or toilet habits have noticeably changed; if you have noticed weight gain or weight loss
- He shows symptoms of bloat, which requires *immediate* attention
- He is salivating excessively
- He has a lump in his throat
- He has a lump or bumps anywhere on the body
- He is very lethargic
- He appears to be in pain or otherwise has trouble chewing or swallowing
- His skin loses elasticity

Of course, there will be other instances in which a visit to the vet is necessary; these are just some of the signs that could be indicative of serious problems that need to be caught as early as possible.

with complicated medical challenges. In most cases, specialists see cases referred by primary-care veterinarians, make diagnoses and set up management plans. From there, the animals' ongoing care is returned to their primary-care veterinarians. This important team approach to your pet's medical-care needs has provided opportunities for advanced care and an unparalleled level of quality to be delivered.

With all of the opportunities for your Field Spaniel to receive high-quality veterinary medical care, there is another topic that needs to be addressed at the same time—cost. It's been said that you can have excellent healthcare or inexpensive healthcare, but never both; this is as true in veterinary medicine as it is in human medicine. While veterinary costs are a fraction of what the same services cost in the human healthcare

FOOD ALLERGY

Severe itching, leading to bald patches and open sores on the feet, face, ears, armpits and groin, could be caused by a food allergy. Studies indicate that up to 10% of dogs suffer from food allergies, which develop slowly over time without a change in diet. Dogs who suffer from chronic ear problems may actually have a food allergy. Unfortunately, there are no tests available to determine whether your dog definitely suffers from a food allergy. The dog will be miserable and you will be frustrated and stressed.

Take the problem into your own hands and kitchen. Select a type of meat that your dog is not getting from his existing diet, perhaps white fish, lamb or venison, and prepare a home-cooked food. The food should consist of two parts carbohydrate (rice, pasta or potatoes) and one part protein (the chosen meat). It's better not to start with soy as the protein source unless all of the meats cause a reaction.

Monitor your dog's intake carefully. He must eat only your prepared meal without any treats or side-trips to the garbage can. All family members (and visiting friends) must be informed of the plan. After four or five weeks on the new diet, you will reintroduce an ingredient from his original diet to determine whether this food is the cause of the skin irritation (or other reactions). Add an ingredient from his old diet about every two weeks and keep careful records of any reactions the dog has to the diet. In this way, you will be able to tell which ingredient from the former diet causes problems for the dog and you can avoid that food in the future.

A vet with experience in sporting breeds, if you can find one, will understand the needs of an active breed who loves the great outdoors.

arena, it is still difficult to deal with unanticipated medical costs, especially since they can easily creep into hundreds or even thousands of dollars if specialists or emergency services become involved. However, there are ways of managing these risks. The easiest is to buy pet health insurance and realize that its foremost purpose is not to cover routine healthcare visits but rather to serve as an umbrella for those rainy days when your pet needs medical care and you don't want to worry about whether or not you can afford that care.

Pet insurance policies are very cost-effective (and very inexpensive by human health-insurance standards), but make sure that you buy the policy long before you intend to use it (preferably starting in puppyhood, because coverage will exclude pre-existing conditions) and that you are actually buying an indemnity insurance plan from an insurance company that is regulated by your state or province. Many insurance policy look-alikes are actually discount clubs that are redeemable only at specific locations and for specific services. An indemnity plan covers your pet at almost all veterinary, specialty and emergency practices and is an excellent way to manage your pet's ongoing healthcare needs.

VACCINATIONS AND INFECTIOUS DISEASES

There has never been an easier time to prevent a variety of infectious diseases in your dog, but the advances we've made in veterinary medicine come with a price—choice. Now while it may seem that this choice is a good thing (and it is), it also has never been more difficult for the pet owner (or the veterinarian) to make an informed decision about the best way to protect pets through vaccination.

Years ago, it was just accepted that puppies got a starter series of vaccinations and then annual "boosters" throughout their lives to keep them protected. As more and more vaccines became available, consumers wanted the convenience of having all of that protection in a single injection. The result was "multivalent" vaccines that crammed a lot of protection into a single syringe. The manufacturers' recommendations were to give the vaccines annually, and this was a simple enough protocol to follow. However, as veterinary medicine has become more sophisticated

Common Infectious Diseases

Let's discuss some of the diseases that create the need for vaccination in the first place. Following are the major canine infectious diseases and a simple explanation of each.

Rabies: A devastating viral disease that can be fatal in dogs and people. In fact, vaccination of dogs and cats is an important public-health measure to create a resistant animal buffer population to protect people from contracting the disease. Vaccination schedules are determined on a government level and are not optional for pet owners; rabies vaccination is required by law in all 50 states.

Parvovirus: A severe, potentially life-threatening disease that is easily transmitted between dogs. There are four strains of the virus, but it is believed that there is significant "cross-protection" between strains that may be included in individual vaccines.

Distemper: A potentially severe and life-threatening disease with a relatively high risk of exposure, especially in certain regions. In very high-risk distemper environments, young pups may be vaccinated with human measles vaccine, a related virus that offers cross-protection when administered at four to ten weeks of age.

Hepatitis: Caused by canine adenovirus type 1 (CAV-1), but since vaccination with the causative virus has a higher rate of adverse effects, cross-protection is derived from the use of adenovirus type 2 (CAV-2), a cause of respiratory disease and one of the potential causes of canine cough. Vaccination with CAV-2 provides long-term immunity against hepatitis, but relatively less protection against respiratory infection.

Canine cough: Also called tracheobronchitis, actually a fairly complicated result of viral and bacterial offenders; therefore, even with vaccination, protection is incomplete. Wherever dogs congregate, canine cough will likely be spread among them. Intranasal vaccination with *Bordetella* and parainfluenza is the best safeguard, but the duration of immunity does not appear to be very long, typically a year at most. These are non-core vaccines, but vaccination is sometimes mandated by boarding kennels, obedience classes, dog shows and other places where dogs congregate to try to minimize spread of infection.

Leptospirosis: A potentially fatal disease that is more common in some geographic regions. It is capable of being spread to humans. The disease varies with the individual "serovar," or strain, of *Leptospira* involved. Since there does not appear to be much cross-protection between serovars, protection is only as good as the likelihood that the serovar in the vaccine is the same as the one in the pet's local environment. Problems with *Leptospira* vaccines are that protection does not last very long, side effects are not uncommon and a large percentage of dogs (perhaps 30%) may not respond to vaccination.

Borrelia burgdorferi: The cause of Lyme disease, the risk of which varies with the geographic area in which the pet lives and travels. Lyme disease is spread by deer ticks in the eastern US and western black-legged ticks in the western part of the country, and the risk of exposure is high in some regions. Lameness, fever and inappetence are most commonly seen in affected dogs. The extent of protection from the vaccine has not been conclusively demonstrated.

Coronavirus: This disease has a high risk of exposure, especially in areas where dogs congregate, but it typically causes only mild to moderate digestive upset (diarrhea, vomiting, etc.). Vaccines are available, but the duration of protection is believed to be relatively short and the effectiveness of the vaccine in preventing infection is considered low.

There are many other vaccinations available, including those for *Giardia* and canine adenovirus-1. While there may be some specific indications for their use, and local risk factors to be considered, they are not widely recommended for most dogs.

and we have started looking more at healthcare quandaries rather than convenience, it became necessary to reevaluate the situation and deal with some tough questions. It is important to realize that whether or not to use a particular vaccine depends on the risk of contracting the disease against which it protects, the severity of the disease if it is contracted, the duration of immunity provided by the vaccine, the safety of the product and the needs of the individual animal. In a very general sense, rabies, distemper, hepatitis and parvovirus are considered core vaccine needs, while parainfluenza, *Bordetella bronchiseptica*, leptospirosis, coronavirus and borreliosis (Lyme disease) are considered non-core needs and best reserved for animals that

The Eyes Have It!

Eye disease is more prevalent among dogs than most people think, ranging from slight infections that are easily treated to serious complications that can lead to permanent sight loss. Eye diseases need veterinary attention in their early stages to prevent irreparable damage. This list provides descriptions of some common eye diseases:

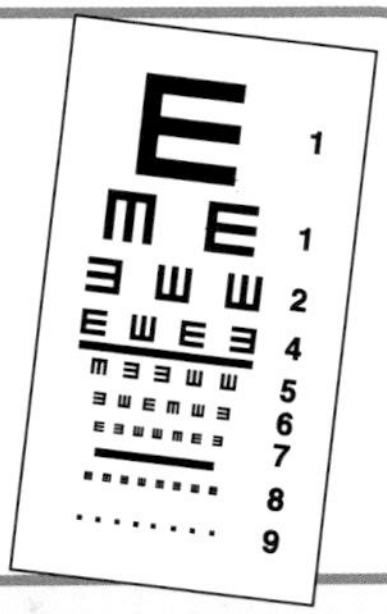

Cataracts: Symptoms are white or gray discoloration of the eye lens and pupil, which causes fuzzy or completely obscured vision. Surgical treatment is required to remove the damaged lens and replace it with an artificial one.

Conjunctivitis: An inflammation of the mucous membrane that lines the eye socket, leaving the eyes red and puffy with excessive discharge. This condition is easily treated with antibiotics.

Corneal damage: The cornea is the transparent covering of the iris and pupil. Injuries are difficult to detect, but manifest themselves in surface abnormality, redness, pain and discharge. Most infections of the cornea are treated with antibiotics and require immediate medical attention.

Dry eye: This condition is caused by deficient production of tears that lubricate and protect the eye surface. A telltale sign is yellow-green discharge. Left undiagnosed, your dog will experience considerable pain, infections and possibly blindness. Dry eye is commonly treated with antibiotics, although more advanced cases may require surgery.

Glaucoma: This is caused by excessive fluid pressure in the eye. Symptoms are red eyes, gray or blue discoloration, pain, enlarged eyeballs and loss of vision. Antibiotics sometimes help, but surgery may be needed.

Dogs, like humans and other animals, can be allergic to airborne substances like pollen, mold spores or fertilizers and pesticides that might be carried their way by the wind.

demonstrate reasonable risk of contracting the diseases.

NEUTERING/SPAYING

Sterilization procedures (neutering for males/spaying for females) are meant to accomplish several purposes. While the underlying premise is to address the risk of pet overpopulation, there are also some medical and behavioral benefits to the surgeries as well. For females, spaying prior to the first estrus (heat cycle) leads to a marked reduction in the risk of mammary cancer and other serious female health problems. There also will be no manifestations of "heat" to attract male dogs and no bleeding in the house. For males, there is prevention of testicular cancer and a reduction in the risk of prostate problems. In both sexes there may be some limited reduction in aggressive behaviors toward other dogs, and some diminishing of urine marking, roaming and mounting.

While neutering and spaying do indeed prevent animals from contributing to pet overpopulation, even no-cost and low-cost neutering options have not eliminated the problem. Perhaps one of the main reasons for this is that individuals that intentionally breed their dogs and those that allow their animals to run at large are the main causes of unwanted offspring. Also, animals in shelters are often there because they were abandoned or relinquished, not because they came from unplanned matings. Neutering/spaying is important, but it should be considered in the context of the real causes of animals' ending up in shelters and eventually being euthanized.

One of the important considerations regarding neutering is that it is a surgical procedure.

This sometimes gets lost in discussions of low-cost procedures and commoditization of the process. In females, spaying is specifically referred to as an ovariohysterectomy. In this procedure, a midline incision is made in the abdomen and the entire uterus and both ovaries are surgically removed. While this is a major invasive surgical procedure, it usually has few complications because it is typically performed on healthy young animals. However, it is major surgery, as any woman who has had a hysterectomy will attest.

In males, neutering has traditionally referred to castration, which involves the surgical removal of both testicles. While still a significant piece of surgery, there is not the abdominal exposure that is required in the female surgery. In addition, there is now a chemical sterilization option, in which a solution is injected into each testicle, leading to atrophy of the sperm-producing cells. This can typically be done under sedation rather than full anesthesia. This is a relatively new approach, and there are no long-term clinical studies yet available.

Neutering/spaying is typically done around six months of age at most veterinary hospitals, although techniques have been pioneered to perform the procedures in animals as young as eight weeks of age. In general, the surgeries on the very young animals are done for the specific reason of sterilizing them before they go to their new homes. This is done in some shelter hospitals for assurance that the animals will definitely not produce any pups. Otherwise, these organizations need to rely on owners to comply with their wishes to have the animals "altered" at a later date, something that does not always happen.

TAKING YOUR DOG'S TEMPERATURE

It is important to know how to take your dog's temperature at times when you think he may be ill. It's not the most enjoyable task, but it can be done without too much difficulty. It's easier with a helper, preferably someone with whom the dog is friendly, so that one of you can hold the dog while the other inserts the thermometer.

Before inserting the thermometer, coat the end with petroleum jelly. Insert the thermometer slowly and gently into the dog's rectum about one inch. Wait for the reading, about two minutes. Be sure to remove the thermometer carefully and clean it thoroughly after each use.

A dog's normal body temperature is between 100.5 and 102.5 degrees F. Immediate veterinary attention is required if the dog's temperature is below 99 or above 104 degrees F.

S. E. M. by Dr. Dennis Kunkel, University of Hawaii.

A scanning electron micrograph of a dog flea, *Ctenocephalides canis*, on dog hair.

EXTERNAL PARASITES

FLEAS

Fleas have been around for millions of years and, while we have better tools now for controlling them than at any time in the past, there still is little chance that they will end up on an endangered species list. Actually, they are very well adapted to living on our pets, and they continue to adapt as we make advances.

The female flea can consume 15 times her weight in blood during active reproduction and can lay as many as 40 eggs a day. These eggs are very resistant to the effects of insecticides. They hatch into larvae, which then mature and spin cocoons. The immature fleas reside in this pupal stage until the time is right for feeding. This pupal stage is also very resistant to the effects of insecticides, and pupae can last in the environment without feeding for many months. Newly emergent fleas are attracted to animals by the warmth of the animals' bodies, movement and exhaled carbon dioxide. However, when they first emerge from their cocoons, they orient towards light; thus when an animal passes between a flea and the light source, casting a shadow, the flea pounces and starts to feed. If the animal turns out to be a dog or cat, the reproductive cycle continues. If the flea lands on another type of animal, including a person, the flea will bite but will then look for a more appropriate host. An emerging adult flea can survive without feeding for up to 12 months but, once it tastes blood, it can survive off its host for only 3 to 4 days.

It was once thought that fleas spend most of their lives in the environment, but we now know that fleas won't willingly jump off a dog unless leaping to another dog or when physically removed by brushing, bathing or other manipulation. Flea eggs, on the other hand, are shiny and smooth, and they roll off the animal and into the environment. The eggs, larvae and pupae then exist in the environment, but once the adult finds a susceptible animal, it's home sweet home until the flea is forced to seek refuge elsewhere.

Since adult fleas live on the animal and immature forms survive in the environment, a successful treatment plan must address all stages of the flea life cycle. There are now several safe and effective flea-control products that can be applied on a monthly basis. These include fipronil, imidacloprid, selamectin and permethrin (found in several formulations). Most of these products have significant flea-killing rates within 24 hours. However, none of them will control the immature forms in the environment. To accomplish this, there are a variety of insect growth regulators that can be sprayed into

FLEA PREVENTION FOR YOUR DOG

- Discuss with your veterinarian the safest product to protect your dog, likely in the form of a monthly tablet or a liquid preparation placed on the back of the dog's neck.
- For dogs suffering from flea-bite dermatitis, a shampoo or topical insecticide treatment is required.
- Your lawn and property should be sprayed with an insecticide designed to kill fleas and ticks that lurk outdoors.
- Using a flea comb, check the dog's coat regularly for any signs of parasites.
- Practice good housekeeping. Vacuum floors, carpets and furniture regularly, especially in the areas that the dog frequents, and wash the dog's bedding weekly.
- Follow up house-cleaning with carpet shampoos and sprays to rid the house of fleas at all stages of development. Insect growth regulators are the safest option.

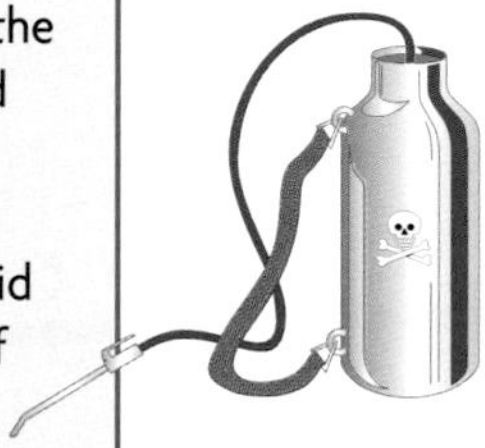

THE FLEA'S LIFE CYCLE

What came first, the flea or the egg? This age-old mystery is more difficult to comprehend than the actual cycle of the flea. Fleas usually live only about four months. A female can lay 2,000 eggs in her lifetime.

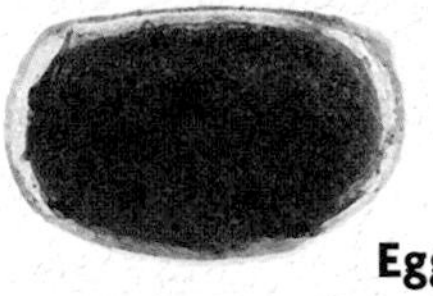

Egg

Photo by Carolina Biological Supply Co.

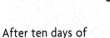

After ten days of rolling around your carpet or under your furniture, the eggs hatch into larvae, which feed on various and sundry debris. In days or months, depending on the climate, the larvae spin cocoons and develop into the pupal or nymph stage, which quickly develop into fleas.

Larva

Photo by Carolina Biological Supply Co.

Pupa

These immature fleas must locate a host within 10 to 14 days or they will die. Only about 1% of the flea population exist as adult fleas, while the other 99% exist as eggs, larvae or pupae.

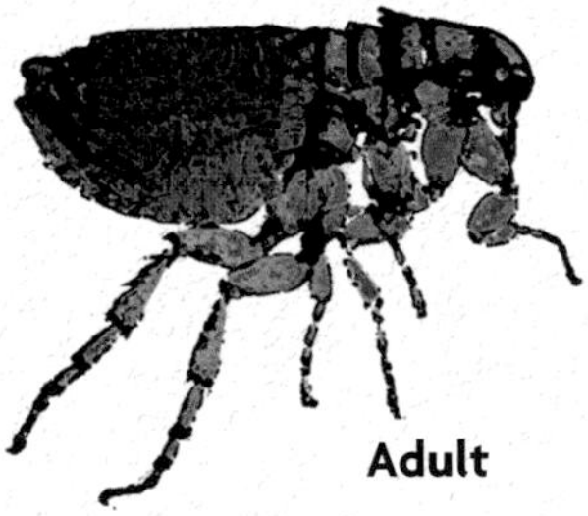

Adult

KILL FLEAS THE NATURAL WAY

If you choose not to go the route of conventional medication, there are some natural ways to ward off fleas:

- Dust your dog with a natural flea powder, composed of such herbal goodies as rosemary, wormwood, pennyroyal, citronella, rue, tobacco powder and eucalyptus.
- Apply diatomaceous earth, the fossilized remains of single-cell algae, to your carpets, furniture and pet's bedding. Even though it's not good for dogs, it's even worse for fleas, which will dry up swiftly and die.
- Brush your dog frequently, give him adequate exercise and let him fast occasionally. All of these activities strengthen the dog's immune system and make him more resistant to disease and parasites.
- Bathe your dog with a capful of pennyroyal or eucalyptus oil.
- Feed a natural diet, free of additives and preservatives. Add some fresh garlic and brewer's yeast to the dog's morning portion, as these items have flea-repelling properties.

the environment (e.g., pyriproxyfen, methoprene, fenoxycarb) as well as insect development inhibitors such as lufenuron that can be administered. These compounds have no effect on adult fleas, but they stop immature forms from developing into adults. In years gone by, we relied heavily on toxic insecticides (such as organophosphates, organochlorines and carbamates) to manage the flea problem, but today's options are not only much safer to use on our pets but also safer for the environment.

TICKS

Ticks are members of the spider class (arachnids) and are bloodsucking parasites capable of transmitting a variety of diseases, including Lyme disease, ehrlichiosis, babesiosis and Rocky Mountain spotted fever. It's easy to see ticks on your own skin, but it is more of a challenge when your furry companion is affected. Whenever you happen to be planning a stroll in a tick-infested area (especially forests, grassy or wooded areas or parks) be prepared to do a thorough inspection of your dog afterward to search for ticks. Ticks can be tricky, so make sure you spend time looking in the ears, between the toes and everywhere else where a tick might hide. Ticks need to be attached for 24–72 hours before they transmit most of the diseases that they carry, so you do have a window of opportunity for some preventive intervention.

A TICKING BOMB

There is nothing good about a tick's harpooning his nose into your dog's skin. Among the diseases caused by ticks are Rocky Mountain spotted fever, canine ehrlichiosis, canine babesiosis, canine hepatozoonosis and Lyme disease. If a dog is allergic to the saliva of a female wood tick, he can develop tick paralysis.

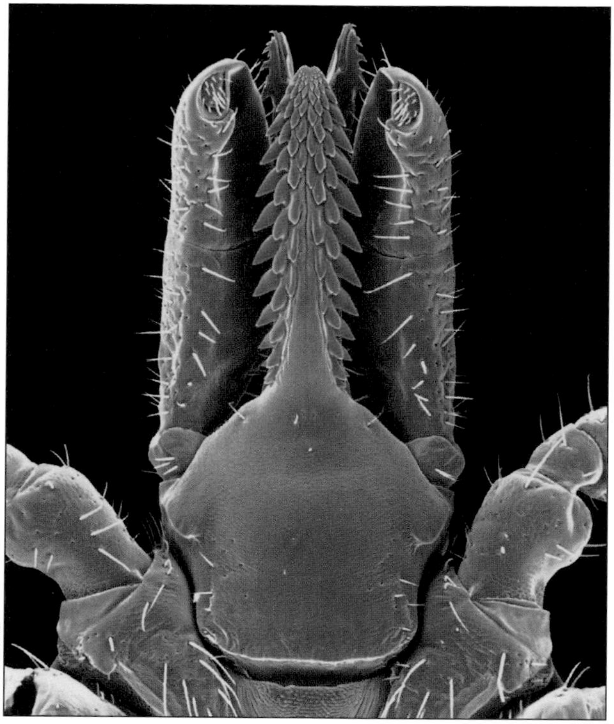

S. E. M. BY PHOTOTAKE.

A scanning electron micrograph of the head of a female deer tick, *Ixodes dammini*, a parasitic tick that carries Lyme disease.

Female ticks live to eat and breed. They can lay between 4,000 and 5,000 eggs and they die soon after. Males, on the other hand, live only to mate with the females and continue the process as long as they are able. Most ticks live on multiple hosts before parasitizing dogs. The immature forms typically reside on grass and shrubs, waiting for susceptible animals to walk by. The larvae and nymph stages typically feed on wildlife.

If only a few ticks are present on a dog, they can be plucked out, but it is important to remove the entire head and mouthparts,

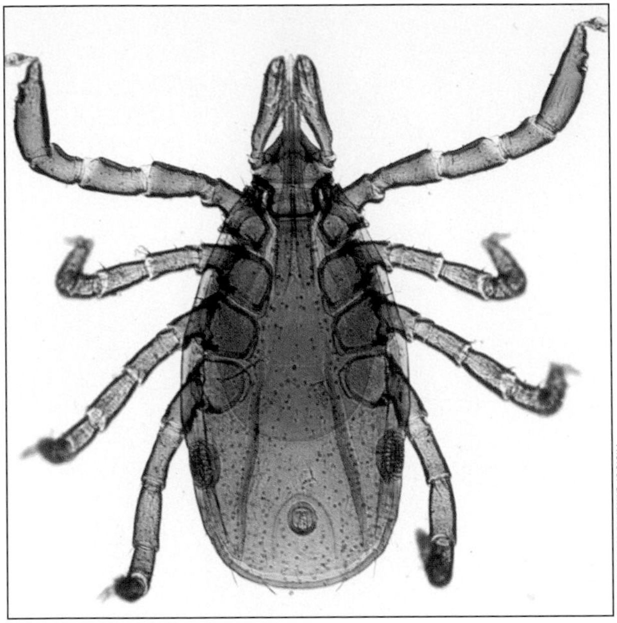

PHOTO BY CAROLINA BIOLOGICAL SUPPLY CO.

Deer tick, *Ixodes dammini.*

which may be deeply embedded in the skin. This is best accomplished with forceps designed especially for this purpose; fingers can be used but should be protected with rubber gloves, plastic wrap or at least a paper towel. The tick should be grasped as closely as possible to the animal's skin and should be pulled upward with steady, even pressure. Do not squeeze, crush or puncture the body of the tick or you risk exposure to any disease carried by that tick. Once the ticks have been removed, the sites of attachment should be disinfected. Your hands should then be washed with soap and water to further minimize risk of contagion. The tick should be disposed of in a container of alcohol or household bleach.

Some of the newer flea products, specifically those with fipronil, selamectin and permethrin, have effect against some, but not all, species of tick. Flea collars containing appropriate pesticides (e.g., propoxur, chlorfenvinphos) can aid in tick control. In most areas, such collars should be placed on animals in March, at the beginning of the tick season, and changed regularly. Leaving the collar on when the pesticide level is waning invites the development of resistance. Amitraz collars are also good for tick control, and the active ingredient does not interfere with other flea-control products. The ingredient helps prevent the attachment of ticks to the skin and will cause those ticks already on the skin to detach themselves.

TICK CONTROL

Removal of underbrush and leaf litter and the thinning of trees in areas where tick control is desired are recommended. These actions remove the cover and food sources for small animals that serve as hosts for ticks. With continued mowing of grasses in these areas, the probability of ticks' surviving is further reduced. A variety of insecticide ingredients (e.g., resmethrin, carbaryl, permethrin, chlorpyrifos, dioxathion and allethrin) are registered for tick control around the home.

Mites

Mites are tiny arachnid parasites that parasitize the skin of dogs. Skin diseases caused by mites are referred to as "mange," and there are many different forms seen in dogs. These forms are very different from one another, each one warranting an individual description.

Sarcoptic mange, or scabies, is one of the itchiest conditions that affects dogs. The microscopic *Sarcoptes* mites burrow into the superficial layers of the skin and can drive dogs crazy with itchiness. They are also communicable to people, although they can't complete their reproductive cycle on people. In addition to being tiny, the mites also are often difficult to find when trying to make a diagnosis. Skin scrapings from multiple areas are examined microscopically but, even then, sometimes the mites cannot be found.

Fortunately, scabies is relatively easy to treat, and there are a variety of products that will successfully kill the mites. Since the mites can't live in the environment for very long without feeding, a complete cure is usually possible within four to eight weeks.

Cheyletiellosis is caused by a relatively large mite, which sometimes can be seen even without a microscope. Often referred to as "walking dandruff," this also causes itching, but not usually as profound as with scabies. While *Cheyletiella* mites can survive somewhat longer in the environment than scabies mites, they too are relatively easy to treat, being responsive to not only the medications used to treat scabies but also often to flea-control products.

Otodectes cynotis is the canine ear mite and is one of the more common causes of mange, especially in young dogs in shelters or pet stores. That's because the mites are typically present in large numbers and are quickly spread to nearby animals. The mites rarely do much harm but

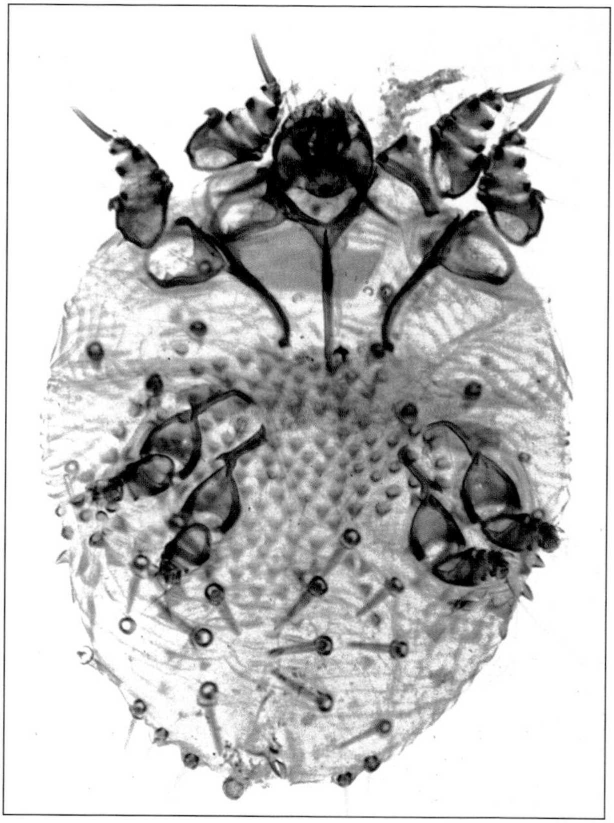

Photo by Phototake.

***Sarcoptes scabiei*, commonly known as the "itch mite."**

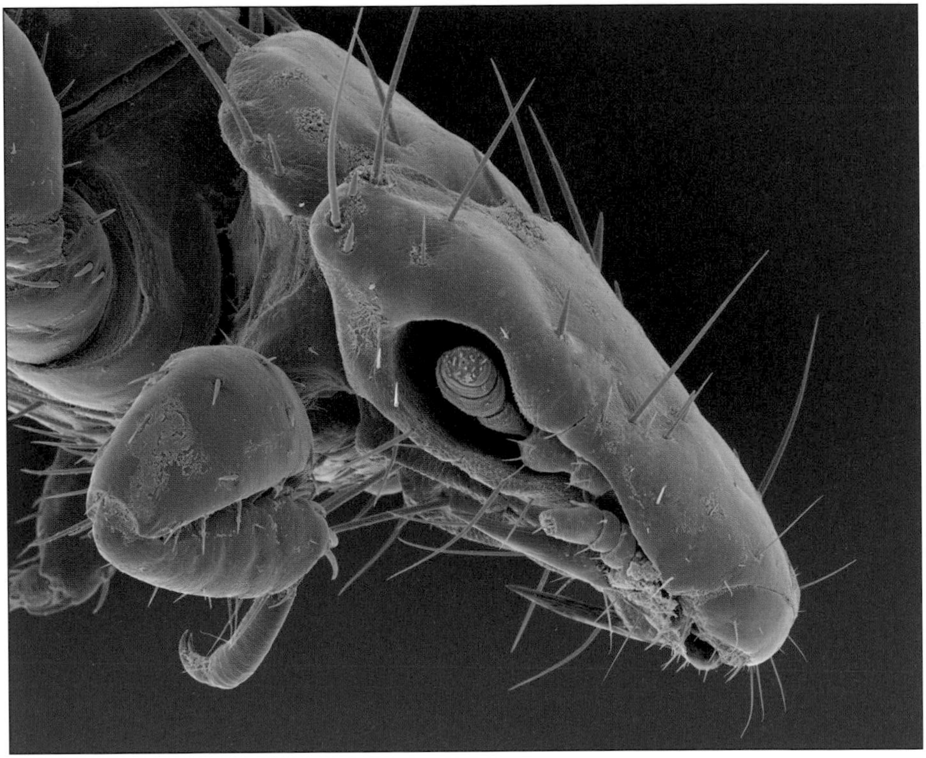

S.E.M. by Dr. Dennis Kunkel, University of Hawaii.

Micrograph of a dog louse, *Heterodoxus spiniger*. Female lice attach their eggs to the hairs of the dog. As the eggs hatch, the larval lice bite and feed on the blood. Lice can also feed on dead skin and hair. This feeding activity can cause hair loss and skin problems.

can be difficult to eradicate if the treatment regimen is not comprehensive. While many try to treat the condition with ear drops only, this is the most common cause of treatment failure. Ear drops cause the mites to simply move out of the ears and as far away as possible (usually to the base of the tail) until the insecticide levels in the ears drop to an acceptable level—then it's back to business as usual! The successful treatment of ear mites requires treating all animals in the household with a systemic insecticide, such as selamectin, or a combination of miticidal ear drops combined with whole-body flea-control preparations.

Demodicosis, sometimes referred to as red mange, can be one of the most difficult forms of mange to treat. Part of the problem has to do with the fact that the mites live in the hair follicles and they are relatively well shielded from topical and systemic products. The main issue, however, is that demodectic mange typically results only when there is some underlying process interfering with the dog's immune system.

Since *Demodex* mites are normal residents of the skin of

mammals, including humans, there is usually a mite population explosion only when the immune system fails to keep the number of mites in check. In young animals, the immune deficit may be transient or may reflect an actual inherited immune problem. In older animals, demodicosis is usually seen only when there is another disease hampering the immune system, such as diabetes, cancer, thyroid problems or the use of immune-suppressing drugs. Accordingly, treatment involves not only trying to kill the mange mites but also discerning what is interfering with immune function and correcting it if possible.

ILLUSTRATION BY PHOTOTAKE.

Illustration of *Demodex folliculoram.*

Chiggers represent several different species of mite that don't parasitize dogs specifically, but do latch on to passersby and can cause irritation. The problem is most prevalent in wooded areas in the late summer and fall. Treatment is not difficult, as the mites do not complete their life cycle on dogs and are susceptible to a variety of miticidal products.

Mosquitoes

Mosquitoes have long been known to transmit a variety of diseases to people, as well as just being biting pests during warm weather. They also pose a real risk to pets. Not only do they carry deadly heartworms but recently there also has been much concern over their involvement with West Nile virus. While we can avoid heartworm with the use of preventive medications, there are no such preventives for West Nile virus. The only method of prevention in endemic areas is active mosquito control. Fortunately, most dogs that have been exposed to the virus only developed flu-like symptoms and, to date, there have not been the large number of reported deaths in canines as seen in some other species.

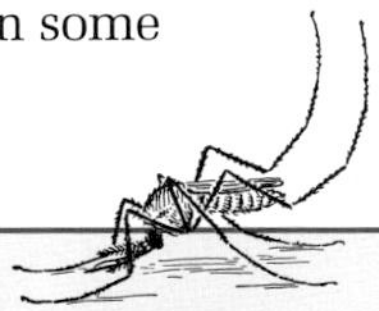

MOSQUITO REPELLENT

Low concentrations of DEET (less than 10%), found in many human mosquito repellents, have been safely used on dogs but, in these concentrations, probably give only about two hours of protection. DEET may be safe in these small concentrations, but since it is not licensed for use on dogs, there is no research proving its safety for dogs. Products containing permethrin give the longest-lasting protection, perhaps two to four weeks. As DEET is not licensed for use on dogs, and both DEET and permethrin can be quite toxic to cats, appropriate care should be exercised. Other products, such as those containing oil of citronella, also have some mosquito-repellent activity, but typically have a relatively short duration of action.

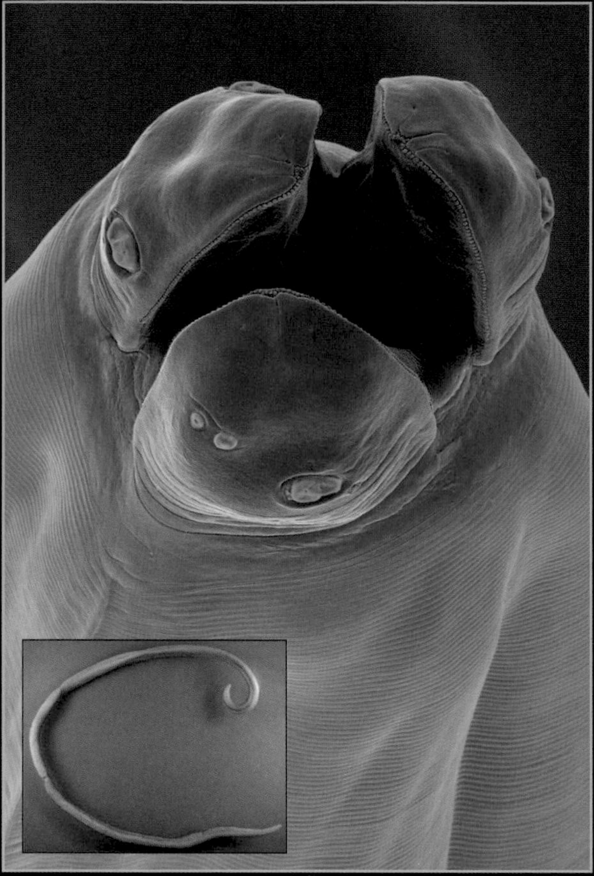

S. E. M. by Dr. Dennis Kunkel, University of Hawaii; Inset by Tam C. Nguyen.

The ascarid roundworm *Toxocara canis*, showing the mouth with three lips. INSET: Photomicrograph of the roundworm *Ascaris lumbricoides*.

ASCARID DANGERS

The most commonly encountered worms in dogs are roundworms known as ascarids. *Toxascaris leonine* and *Toxocara canis* are the two species that infect dogs. Subsisting in the dog's stomach and intestines, adult roundworms can grow to 7 inches in length and adult females can lay in excess of 200,000 eggs in a single day.

In humans, visceral larval migrans affects people who have ingested eggs of *Toxocara canis*, which frequently contaminates children's sandboxes, beaches and park grounds. The roundworms reside in the human's stomach and intestines, as they would in a dog's, but do not mature. Instead, they find their way to the liver, lungs and skin, or even to the heart or kidneys in severe cases. Deworming puppies is critical in preventing the infection in humans, and young children should never handle nursing pups who have not been dewormed.

INTERNAL PARASITES: WORMS

Ascarids

Ascarids are intestinal roundworms that rarely cause severe disease in dogs. Nonetheless, they are of major public health significance because they can be transferred to people. Sadly, it is children who are most commonly affected by the parasite, probably from inadvertently ingesting ascarid-contaminated soil. In fact, many yards and children's sandboxes contain appreciable numbers of ascarid eggs. So, while ascarids don't bite dogs or latch onto their intestines to suck blood, they do cause some nasty medical conditions in children and are best eradicated from our furry friends. Because pups can start passing ascarid eggs by three weeks of age, most parasite-control programs begin at two weeks of age and are repeated every two weeks until pups are eight weeks old. It is important to

HOOKED ON *ANCYLOSTOMA*

Adult dogs can become infected by the bloodsucking nematodes we commonly call hookworms via ingesting larvae from the ground or via the larvae penetrating the dog's skin. It is not uncommon for infected dogs to show no symptoms of hookworm infestation. Sometimes symptoms occur within ten days of exposure. These symptoms can include bloody diarrhea, anemia, loss of weight and general weakness. Dogs pass the hookworm eggs in their stools, which serves as the vet's method of identifying the infestation. The hookworm larvae can encyst themselves in the dog's tissues and be released when the dog is experiencing stress.

Caused by an *Ancylostoma* species whose common host is the dog, cutaneous larval migrans affects humans, causing itching and lumps and streaks beneath the surface of the skin.

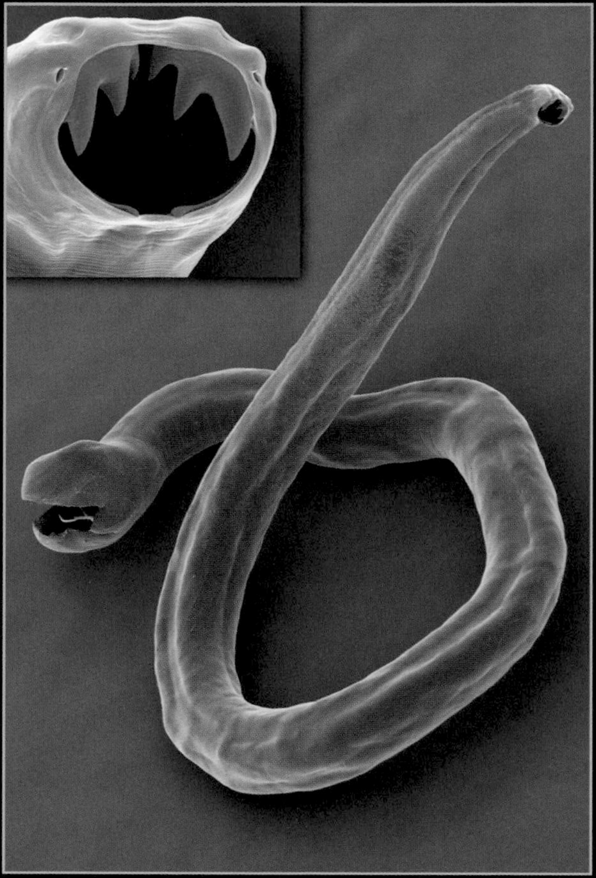

S. E. M. by Dr. Dennis Kunkel, University of Hawaii.

The hookworm *Ancylostoma caninum* infests the intestines of dogs. INSET: Note the row of hooks at the posterior end, used to anchor the worm to the intestinal wall.

realize that bitches can pass ascarids to their pups even if they test negative prior to whelping. Accordingly, bitches are best treated at the same time as the pups.

HOOKWORMS

Unlike ascarids, hookworms do latch onto a dog's intestinal tract and can cause significant loss of blood and protein. Similar to ascarids, hookworms can be transmitted to humans, where they cause a condition known as cutaneous larval migrans. Dogs can become infected either by consuming the infective larvae or by the larvae's penetrating the skin directly. People most often get infected when they are lying on the ground (such as on a beach) and the larvae penetrate the skin. Yes, the larvae can penetrate through a beach blanket. Hookworms are typically susceptible to the same medications used to treat ascarids.

Whipworms

Whipworms latch onto the lower aspects of the dog's colon and can cause cramping and diarrhea. Eggs do not start to appear in the dog's feces until about three months after the dog was infected. This worm has a peculiar life cycle, which makes it more difficult to control than ascarids or hookworms. The good thing is that whipworms rarely are transferred to people.

Some of the medications used to treat ascarids and hookworms are also effective against whipworms, but, in general, a separate treatment protocol is needed. Since most of the medications are effective against the adults but not the eggs or larvae, treatment is typically repeated in three weeks, and then often in three months as well. Unfortunately, since dogs don't develop resistance to whipworms, it is difficult to prevent them from getting reinfected if they visit soil contaminated with whipworm eggs.

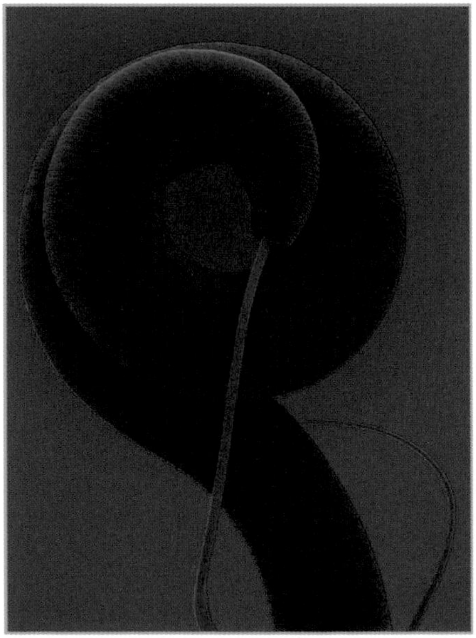

Adult whipworm, *Trichuris* sp., an intestinal parasite.

S.E.M. by Dr. Dennis Kunkel, University of Hawaii.

WORM-CONTROL GUIDELINES

- Practice sanitary habits with your dog and home.
- Clean up after your dog and don't let him sniff or eat other dogs' droppings.
- Control insects and fleas in the dog's environment. Fleas, lice, cockroaches, beetles, mice and rats can act as hosts for various worms.
- Prevent dogs from eating uncooked meat, raw poultry and dead animals.
- Keep dogs and children from playing in sand and soil.
- Kennel dogs on cement or gravel; avoid dirt runs.
- Administer heartworm preventives regularly.
- Have your vet examine your dog's stools at your annual visits.
- Select a boarding kennel carefully so as to avoid contamination from other dogs or an unsanitary environment.
- Prevent dogs from roaming. Obey local leash laws.

Tapeworms

There are many different species of tapeworm that affect dogs, but *Dipylidium caninum* is probably the most common and is spread by fleas. Flea larvae feed on organic debris and tapeworm eggs in the environment and, when a dog chews at himself and manages to ingest fleas, he might get a dose of tapeworm at the same time. The tapeworm then develops further in the intestine of the dog.

The tapeworm itself, which is a parasitic flatworm that latches onto the intestinal wall, is composed of numerous segments. When the segments break off into the intestine (as proglottids), they may accumulate around the rectum, like grains of rice. While this tapeworm is disgusting in its behavior, it is not directly communicable to humans (although humans can also get infected by swallowing fleas).

S. E. M. by Dr. Dennis Kunkel, University of Hawaii.

A dog tapeworm proglottid (body segment).

A much more dangerous flatworm is *Echinococcus multilocularis*, which is typically found in foxes, coyotes and wolves. The eggs are passed in the feces and infect rodents, and, when dogs eat the rodents, the dogs can be infected by thousands of adult tapeworms. While the parasites don't cause many problems in dogs, this is considered the most lethal worm infection that people can get. Take appropriate precautions if you live in an area in which these tapeworms are found. Do not use mulch that may contain feces of dogs, cats or wildlife, and discourage your pets from hunting wildlife. Treat these tapeworm infections aggressively in pets, because if humans get infected, approximately half die.

Heartworms

Heartworm disease is caused by the parasite *Dirofilaria immitis* and is seen in dogs around the world. A member of the roundworm group, it is spread between dogs by the bite of an infected mosquito. The mosquito injects infective larvae into the dog's skin with its bite, and these larvae develop under the skin for a period of time before making their way to the heart. There they develop into adults, which grow and create blockages of the heart, lungs and major blood vessels there. They also start producing offspring (microfilariae),

S. E. M. by Dr. Dennis Kunkel, University of Hawaii.

The dog tapeworm *Taenia pisiformis*.

A Look at Internal Parasites

Photo by Carolina Biological Supply Co.

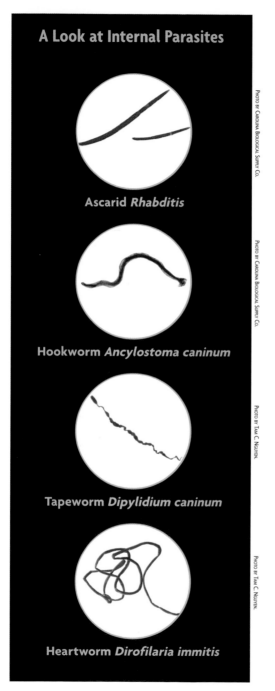

Ascarid *Rhabditis*

Photo by Carolina Biological Supply Co.

Hookworm *Ancylostoma caninum*

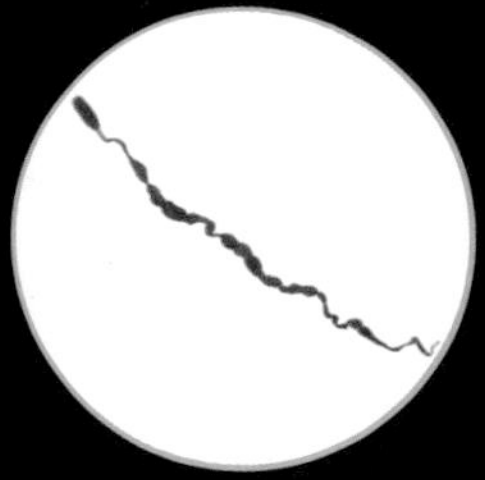

Photo by Tam C. Nguyen.

Tapeworm *Dipylidium caninum*

Photo by Tam C. Nguyen.

Heartworm *Dirofilaria immitis*

and these microfilariae circulate in the bloodstream, waiting to hitch a ride when the next mosquito bites. Once in the mosquito, the microfilariae develop into infective larvae and the entire process is repeated.

When dogs get infected with heartworm, over time they tend to develop symptoms associated with heart disease, such as coughing, exercise intolerance and potentially many other manifestations. Diagnosis is confirmed by either seeing the microfilariae themselves in blood samples or using immunologic tests (antigen testing) to identify the presence of adult heartworms. Since antigen tests measure the presence of adult heartworms and microfilarial tests measure offspring produced by adults, neither are positive until six to seven months after the initial infection. However, the beginning of damage can occur by fifth-stage larvae as early as three months after infection. Thus it is possible for dogs to be harboring problem-causing larvae for up to three months before either type of test would identify an infection.

The good news is that there are great protocols available for preventing heartworm in dogs. Testing is critical in the process, and it is important to understand the benefits as well as the limitations of such testing. All dogs six months of age or older that have not been on continuous heartworm-preventive medication should be

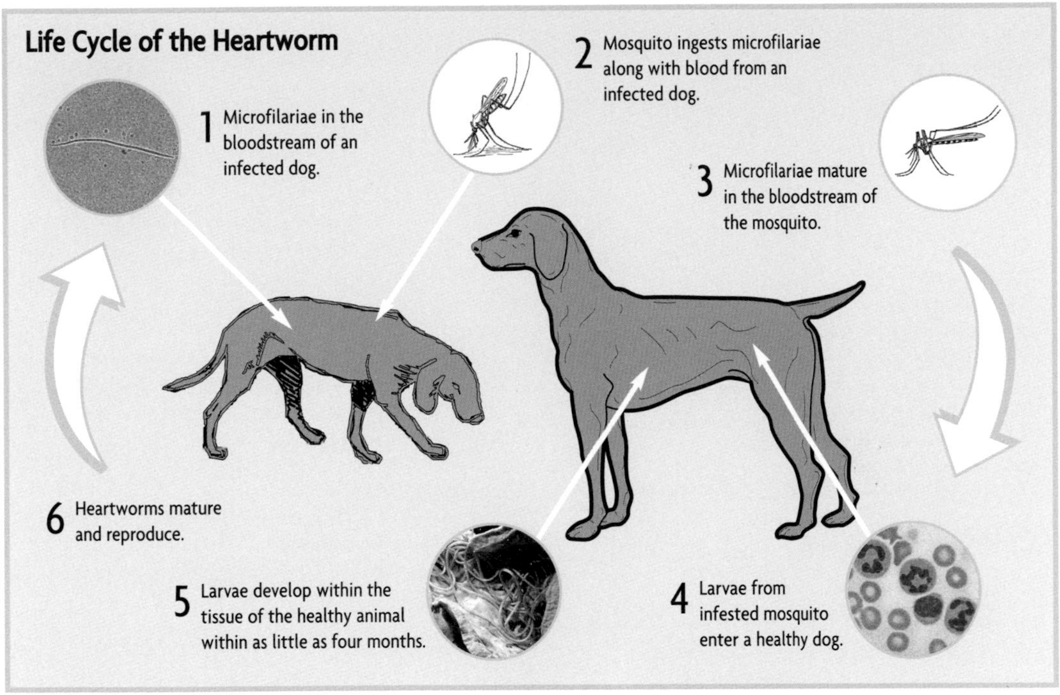
Life Cycle of the Heartworm
1 Microfilariae in the bloodstream of an infected dog.
2 Mosquito ingests microfilariae along with blood from an infected dog.
3 Microfilariae mature in the bloodstream of the mosquito.
4 Larvae from infested mosquito enter a healthy dog.
5 Larvae develop within the tissue of the healthy animal within as little as four months.
6 Heartworms mature and reproduce.

screened with microfilarial or antigen tests. For dogs receiving preventive medication, periodic antigen testing helps assess the effectiveness of the preventives. The American Heartworm Society guidelines suggest that annual retesting may not be necessary when owners have absolutely provided continuous heartworm prevention. Retesting on a two- to three-year interval may be sufficient in these cases. However, your veterinarian will likely have specific guidelines under which heartworm preventives will be prescribed, and many prefer to err on the side of safety and retest annually.

It is indeed fortunate that heartworm is relatively easy to prevent, because treatments can be as life-threatening as the disease itself. Treatment requires a two-step process that kills the adult heartworms first and then the microfilariae. Prevention is obviously preferable; this involves a once-monthly oral or topical treatment. The most common oral preventives include ivermectin (not suitable for some breeds), moxidectin and milbemycin oxime; the once-a-month topical drug selamectin provides heartworm protection in addition to flea, some types of tick and other parasite controls.

THE ABCs OF Emergency Care

Abrasions
Clean wound with running water or 3% hydrogen peroxide. Pat dry with gauze and spray with antibiotic. Do not cover.

Animal Bites
Clean area with soap and saline solution or water. Apply pressure to any bleeding area. Apply antibiotic ointment. Identify biting animal and contact the vet.

Antifreeze Poisoning
Induce vomiting and take dog to the vet.

Bee Sting
Remove stinger and apply soothing lotion or cold compress; give antihistamine in proper dosage.

Bleeding
Apply pressure directly to wound with gauze or towel for five to ten minutes. If wound does not stop bleeding, wrap wound with gauze and adhesive tape.

Bloat/Gastric Torsion
Immediately take the dog to the vet or emergency clinic; phone from car. No time to waste.

Burns
Chemical: Bathe dog with water and pet shampoo. Rinse in saline solution. Apply antibiotic ointment.

Acid: Rinse with water. Apply one part baking soda, two parts water to affected area.

Alkali: Rinse with water. Apply one part vinegar, four parts water to affected area.

Electrical: Apply antibiotic ointment. Seek veterinary assistance immediately.

Choking
If the dog is on the verge of collapsing, wedge a solid object, such as the handle of a screwdriver, between molars on one side of mouth to keep mouth open. Pull tongue out. Use long-nosed pliers or fingers to remove foreign object. Do not push the object down the dog's throat. For small or medium dogs, hold dog upside down by hind legs and shake firmly to dislodge foreign object.

Chlorine Ingestion
With clean water, rinse the mouth and eyes. Give dog water to drink; contact the vet.

Constipation
Feed dog 2 tablespoons bran flakes with each meal. Encourage drinking water. Mix ¼-teaspoon mineral oil in dog's food. Contact vet if persists longer than 24 hours.

Diarrhea
Withhold food for 12 to 24 hours. Feed dog anti-diarrheal with eyedropper. When feeding resumes, feed one part boiled hamburger, one part plain cooked rice, ¼ to ¾-cup four times daily. Contact vet if persists longer than 24 hours.

Dog Bite
Snip away hair around puncture wound; clean with 3% hydrogen peroxide; apply tincture of iodine. Identify biting dog and call the vet. If wound appears deep, take the dog to the vet.

Frostbite
Wrap the dog in a heavy blanket. Warm affected area with a warm bath for ten minutes. Red color to skin will return with circulation; if tissues are pale after 20 minutes, contact the vet.

Use a portable, durable container large enough to contain all items.

Heat Stroke
Submerge the dog (up to his muzzle) in cold water; if no response within ten minutes, contact the vet.

Hot Spots
Mix 2 packets Domeboro® with 2 cups water. Saturate cloth with mixture and apply to hot spots for 15–30 minutes. Apply antibiotic ointment. Repeat every six to eight hours.

Poisonous Plants
Wash affected area with soap and water. Cleanse with alcohol. For foxtail/grass, apply antibiotic ointment. Contact vet if plant was ingested.

Rat Poison Ingestion
Induce vomiting. Keep dog calm, maintain dog's normal body temperature (use blanket or heating pad). Get to the vet for antidote.

Shock
Keep the dog calm and warm; call for veterinary assistance.

Snake Bite
If possible, bandage the area and apply pressure. If the area is not conducive to bandaging, use ice to control bleeding. Get immediate help from the vet.

Tick Removal
Apply flea and tick spray directly on tick. Wait one minute. Using tweezers or wearing plastic gloves, grasp the tick's body firmly. Apply antibiotic ointment.

Vomiting
Restrict water intake; offer a few ice cubes. Withhold food for next meal. Contact vet if vomiting persists longer than 24 hours.

DOG OWNER'S FIRST-AID KIT

- ❑ Gauze bandages/swabs
- ❑ Adhesive and non-adhesive bandages
- ❑ Antibiotic powder
- ❑ Antiseptic wash
- ❑ Hydrogen peroxide 3%
- ❑ Antibiotic ointment
- ❑ Lubricating jelly
- ❑ Rectal thermometer
- ❑ Nylon muzzle
- ❑ Scissors and forceps
- ❑ Eyedropper
- ❑ Syringe
- ❑ Anti-bacterial/fungal solution
- ❑ Saline solution
- ❑ Antihistamine
- ❑ Cotton balls
- ❑ Nail clippers
- ❑ Screwdriver/pen knife
- ❑ Flashlight
- ❑ Emergency phone numbers

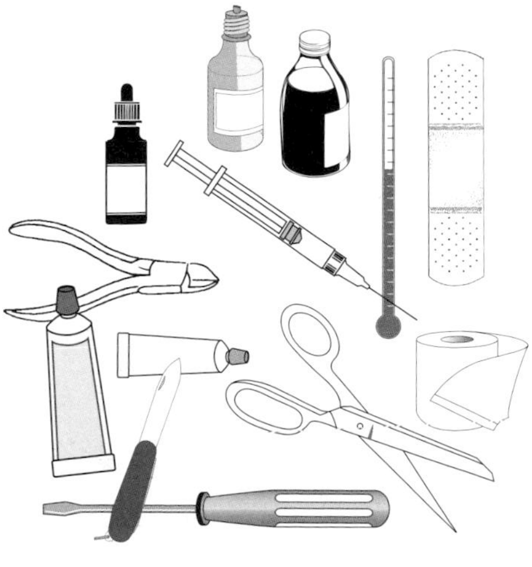

Number-One Killer Disease in Dogs: CANCER

In every age, there is a word associated with a disease or plague that causes humans to shudder. In the 21st century, that word is "cancer." Just as cancer is the leading cause of death in humans, it claims nearly half the lives of dogs that die from a natural disease as well as half the dogs that die over the age of ten years.

Described as a genetic disease, cancer becomes a greater risk as the dog ages. Vets and dog owners have become increasingly aware of the threat of cancer to dogs. Statistics reveal that one dog in every five will develop cancer, the most common of which is skin cancer. Many cancers, including prostate, ovarian and breast cancer, can be avoided by spaying and neutering our dogs by the age of six months.

Early detection of cancer can save or extend a dog's life, so it is absolutely vital for owners to have their dogs examined by a qualified vet or oncologist immediately upon detection of any abnormality. Certain dietary guidelines have also proven to reduce the onset and spread of cancer. Foods based on fish rather than beef, due to the presence of Omega-3 fatty acids, are recommended. Other amino acids such as glutamine have significant benefits for canines, particularly those breeds that show a greater susceptibility to cancer.

Cancer management and treatments promise hope for future generations of canines. Since the disease is genetic, breeders should never breed a dog whose parents, grandparents and any related siblings have developed cancer. It is difficult to know whether to exclude an otherwise healthy dog from a breeding program, as the disease does not manifest itself until the dog's senior years.

RECOGNIZE CANCER WARNING SIGNS

Since early detection can possibly rescue your dog from becoming a cancer statistic, it is essential for owners to recognize the possible signs and seek the assistance of a qualified professional.

- Abnormal bumps or lumps that continue to grow
- Bleeding or discharge from any body cavity
- Persistent stiffness or lameness
- Recurrent sores or sores that do not heal
- Inappetence
- Breathing difficulties
- Weight loss
- Bad breath or odors
- General malaise and fatigue
- Eating and swallowing problems
- Difficulty urinating and defecating

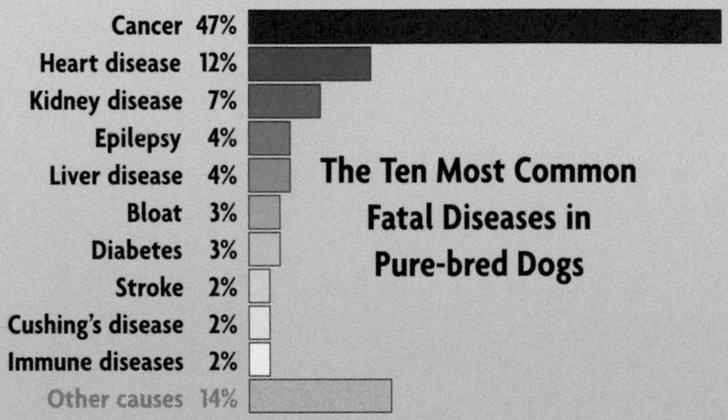

The Ten Most Common Fatal Diseases in Pure-bred Dogs

YOUR SENIOR

FIELD SPANIEL

WHEN IS MY DOG A "SENIOR"?

Field Spaniels have an average lifespan of approximately 14 years (range of 12 to 16 years), which is considerable for any pure-bred dog, regardless of size, lineage or utility. The typical age at which a dog is considered a "senior" varies greatly. It is probably safe to say that by age 12 years, most Field Spaniels are retired or semi-retired from strenuous physical activities. Keeping an aging Field Spaniel active within reason is recommended for both mental and physical well-being.

Obviously, the old "seven dog years to one human year" theory is not exact. In puppyhood, a dog's year is actually comparable to more than seven human years, considering the puppy's rapid growth during his first year. Then, in adulthood, the ratio decreases. Regardless, the more viable rule of thumb is that the larger the dog, the shorter his expected lifespan. Of course, this can vary among individual dogs, with many living longer than expected, which we hope is the case!

WHAT ARE THE SIGNS OF AGING?

By the time your dog has reached his senior years, you will know him very well, so the physical and behavioral changes that accompany aging should be noticeable to you. Humans and dogs share the most obvious physical sign of aging: gray hair! Graying often occurs first on the muzzle and face, around the eyes. Other telltale signs are the dog's overall decrease in activity. Your older dog might be more content to nap and rest, and he may not show the same old enthusiasm when it's time to play

WHAT A RELIEF!

Much like young puppies, older dogs do not have as much control over their excretory functions as they do as non-seniors. Their muscle control fades and, as such, they cannot "hold it" for as long as they used to. This is easily remedied by additional trips outside. If your dog's sight is failing, have the yard well lit at night and/or lead him to his relief site on lead. Incontinence should be discussed with your vet.

CAUSES OF CHANGE

Cognitive dysfunction may not be the cause of all changes in your older dog; illness and medication can also affect him. Things like diabetes, Cushing's disease, cancer and brain tumors are serious physical problems but can cause behavioral changes as well. Older dogs are more prone to these conditions, which should not be overlooked as possibilities for your dog's acting not like his "old self." Any significant changes in your senior's behavior are good reasons to take your dog to the vet for a thorough exam.

Your dog's reactions to medication can cause changes as well. The various types of corticosteroids are often cited as affecting a dog's behavior. If your vet prescribes any type of drug, discuss possible side effects before administering the medication to your dog.

in the yard or go for a walk. Other physical signs include significant weight loss or gain; more labored movement; skin and coat problems, possibly hair loss; sight and/or hearing problems; changes in toileting habits, perhaps seeming "unhousebroken" at times; and tooth decay, bad breath or other mouth problems.

There are behavioral changes that go along with aging, too. There are numerous causes for behavioral changes. Sometimes a dog's apparent confusion results from a physical change like diminished sight or hearing. If his confusion causes him to be afraid, he may act aggressively or defensively. He may sleep more frequently because his daily walks, though shorter now, tire him out. He may begin to experience separation anxiety or, conversely, become less interested in petting and attention.

There also are clinical conditions that cause behavioral changes in older dogs. One such condition is known as canine cognitive dysfunction (familiarly known as "old-dog" syndrome). It can be frustrating for an owner whose dog is affected with cognitive dysfunction, as it can result in behavioral changes of all types, most seemingly unexplainable. Common changes include the dog's forgetting aspects of the daily routine, such as times to eat, go out for walks, relieve himself and the like. Along the same lines, you may take your dog out at the regular time for a potty trip and he may have no idea why he is there. Sometimes a placid dog will begin to show aggressive or possessive tendencies or, conversely, a hyperactive dog will start to "mellow out."

Disease also can be the cause of behavioral changes in senior dogs. Hormonal problems

(Cushing's disease is common in older dogs), diabetes and thyroid disease can cause increased appetite, which can lead to aggression related to food guarding. It's better to be proactive with your senior dog, making more frequent trips to the vet if necessary and having bloodwork done to test for the diseases that can commonly befall older dogs.

This is not to say that, as dogs age, they all fall apart physically and become nasty in personality. The aforementioned changes are discussed to alert owners to the things that may happen as their dogs get older. Many hardy dogs remain active and alert well into old age. However, it can be frustrating and heartbreaking for owners to see their beloved dogs change physically and temperamentally. Just know that it's the same Field Spaniel under there, and that he still loves you and appreciates your care, which he needs now more than ever.

HOW DO I CARE FOR MY AGING DOG?

Again, every dog is an individual in terms of aging. Your dog might advance in years and show no signs of slowing down. However, even if he shows no outward signs of aging, he should begin a senior-care program as determined by the vet. He may not show it, but he's not a pup anymore! Many vets use the seven- or eight-year mark as a time to start a preventive senior-healthcare program. By providing your Field Spaniel with extra attention to his veterinary care,

AH, MY ACHING BONES!

As your pet ages and things that once were routine become difficult for him to handle, you may need to make some adjustments around the home to make things easier for your dog. Senior dogs affected by arthritis may have trouble moving about. If you notice this in your dog, you may have to limit him to one floor of the house so that he does not have to deal with stairs. If there are a few steps leading out into the yard, a ramp may help the dog. Likewise, he may need a ramp or a boost to get in and out of the car. Ensure that he has plenty of soft bedding on which to sleep and rest, as this will be comfortable for his aching joints. Also ensure that surfaces on which the dog walks are not slippery.

Investigate new dietary supplements made for arthritic dogs. Studies have found that products containing glucosamine added once or twice daily to the senior dog's food can have beneficial effects on the dog's joints. Many of these products also contain natural anti-inflammatories such as chondroitin, MSM and cetyl myristoleate, as well as natural herbal remedies and nutmeg. Talk to your vet about these supplements.

ADAPTING TO AGE

As dogs age and their once-keen senses begin to deteriorate, they can experience stress and confusion. However, dogs are very adaptable, and most can adjust to deficiencies in their sight and hearing. As these processes often deteriorate gradually, the dog makes adjustments gradually, too. Because dogs become so familiar with the layout of their homes and yards, and with their daily routines, they are able to get around even if they cannot see or hear as well. Help your senior dog by keeping things consistent around the house. Keep up with your regular times for walking and potty trips, and do not relocate his crate or rearrange the furniture. Your dog is a very adaptable creature and can make compensation for his diminished ability, but you want to help him along the way and not make changes that will cause him confusion.

you will be practicing good preventive medicine, ensuring that the rest of your dog's life will be as long, active, happy and healthy as possible. If you do notice indications of aging, such as graying and/or changes in sleeping, eating or toileting habits, this is a sign to set up a senior-care visit with your vet right away to make sure that these changes are not related to any health problems.

To start, senior dogs should visit the vet twice yearly for exams, routine tests and overall evaluations. Many veterinarians have special screening programs especially for senior dogs that can include a thorough physical exam; blood test to determine complete blood count; serum biochemistry test, which screens for liver, kidney and blood problems as well as cancer; urinalysis; and dental exams. With these tests, it can be determined whether your dog has any health problems; the results also establish a baseline for your pet against which future test results can be compared.

In addition to these tests, your vet may suggest additional testing, including an EKG, tests for glaucoma and other problems of the eye, chest X-rays, screening for tumors, blood pressure test, test for thyroid function and screening for parasites and reassessment of his preventive program. Your vet also will ask you questions about your dog's diet and activity level, what you feed and the amounts that you feed. This information, along with his evaluation of the dog's overall condition, will enable him to suggest proper dietary changes, if needed.

This may seem like quite a work-up for your pet, but veterinarians advise that older dogs need more frequent attention so that any health problems can be detected as early as possible. Serious conditions like kidney disease, heart disease and cancer may not present outward symptoms, or the problem may go undetected if the symptoms are mistaken by owners as just part of the aging process.

There are some conditions more common in elderly dogs that are difficult to ignore. Cognitive dysfunction shares much in common with senility and Alzheimer's disease, and dogs are not immune. Dogs can become confused and/or disoriented, lose their house-training, have abnormal sleep-wake cycles and interact differently with their owners. Be heartened by the fact that, in some ways, there are more treatment options for dogs with cognitive dysfunction than for people with similar conditions. There is good evidence that continued stimulation in the form of games, play, training and exercise can help to maintain cognitive function. There are also medications (such as seligiline) and antioxidant-fortified senior diets that have been shown to be beneficial.

Cancer is also a condition more common in the elderly. Although lung cancer, which is a major killer in humans, is relatively rare in dogs, almost all of the cancers seen in people are also seen in pets. If pets are getting regular physical examinations, cancers are often detected early. There are a variety of cancer therapies available today, and many pets continue to live happy lives with appropriate treatment.

Degenerative joint disease, often referred to as arthritis, is another malady common to both elderly dogs and humans. A lifetime of wear and tear on joints and running around at play eventually takes its toll and results in stiffness and difficulty in getting around. As dogs live longer and healthier lives, it is natural that they should eventually feel some of the effects of aging. Once again, if your Field Spaniel has had regular veterinary care, then he should not have been carrying

WEATHER WORRIES

Older pets are less tolerant of extremes in weather, both heat and cold. Your older dog should not spend extended periods in the sun; when outdoors in the warm weather, make sure he does not become overheated. In chilly weather, consider a sweater for your dog when outdoors and limit time spent outside. Whether or not his coat is thinning, he will need provisions to keep him warm when the weather is cold. Make sure that his bed is placed in a warm area, away from chills and drafts.

ACCIDENT ALERT!

Just as we puppy-proof our homes for the new member of the family, we must accident-proof our homes for the older dog. You want to create a safe environment in which the senior dog can get around easily and comfortably, with no dangers. A dog that slips and falls in old age is much more prone to injury than an adult, making accident prevention even more important. Likewise, dogs are more prone to falls in old age, as they do not have the same balance and coordination that they once had. Throw rugs on hardwood floors are slippery and pose a risk; even a throw rug on a carpeted surface can be an obstacle for the senior dog. Consider putting down non-slip surfaces or confining your dog to carpeted rooms only.

extra pounds all those years and wearing those joints out before their time. If your pet was unfortunate enough to inherit hip dysplasia, osteochondritis dissecans or any of the other developmental orthopedic diseases, battling the onset of degenerative joint disease was probably a longstanding goal. In any case, there are now many effective remedies for managing degenerative joint disease and a number of remarkable surgeries as well.

Aside from the extra veterinary care, there is much you can do at home to keep your older dog in good condition. The dog's diet is an important factor. If your dog's appetite decreases, he will not be getting the nutrients he needs. He also will lose weight, which is unhealthy for a dog at a proper weight. Conversely, an older dog's metabolism is slower and he usually exercises less, but he should not be allowed to become obese. Obesity in an older dog is especially risky, because extra pounds mean extra stress on the body, increasing his vulnerability to heart disease. Additionally, the extra pounds make it harder for the dog to move about.

You should discuss age-related feeding changes with your vet. For a dog who has lost interest in food, it may be suggested to try some different types of food until you find something new that the dog likes. For an obese dog, a "light"-formula dog food or reducing food portions may be advised, along with exercise appropriate to his physical condition and energy level.

As for exercise, the senior dog should not be allowed to become a "couch potato" despite his old age. He may not be able to handle the morning run, long walks and vigorous games of fetch, but he still needs to get up and get moving. Keep up with your daily walks, but keep the distances shorter and let your dog set the pace. If he gets to the point where he's not up for walks, let him stroll around the yard. On the other hand, many dogs remain very active in their senior years, so base changes to the exercise program on your own individual dog and what he's capable of. Don't worry, your Field Spaniel will let you know when it's time to rest.

Keep up with your grooming routine as you always have. Be extra-diligent about checking the skin and coat for problems. Older dogs can experience thinning coats as a normal aging process, but they can also lose hair as a result of medical problems. Some thinning is normal, but patches of baldness or the loss of significant amounts of hair is not.

Hopefully, you've been regular with brushing your dog's teeth throughout his life. Healthy teeth directly affect overall good health. We already know that bacteria from gum infections can enter the dog's body through the damaged gums and travel to the organs. At a stage in life when his organs don't function as well as they used to, you don't want anything to put additional strain on them. Clean teeth also contribute to a healthy immune system. Offering the dental-type chews in addition to toothbrushing can help, as they remove plaque and tartar as the dog chews.

Along with the same good care you've given him all of his life, pay a little extra attention to your dog in his senior years and keep up with twice-yearly trips to the vet. The sooner a problem is uncovered, the greater the chances of a full recovery.

RUBDOWN REMEDY

A good remedy for an aching dog is to give him a gentle massage each day, or even a few times a day if possible. This can be especially beneficial before your dog gets out of his bed in the morning. Just as in humans, massages can decrease pain in dogs, whether the dog is arthritic or just afflicted by the stiffness that accompanies old age. Gently massage his joints and limbs, as well as petting him on his entire body. This can help his circulation and flexibility and ease any joint or muscle aches. Massaging your dog has benefits for you, too; in fact, just petting our dogs can cause reduced levels of stress and lower our blood pressure. Massage and petting also help you find any previously undetected lumps, bumps or abnormalities. Often these are not visible and only turn up by being felt.

SHOWING YOUR
FIELD SPANIEL

Is dog showing in your blood? Are you excited by the idea of gaiting your handsome Field Spaniel around the ring to the thunderous applause of an enthusiastic audience? Are you certain that your beloved Field Spaniel is flawless? You are not alone! Every loving owner thinks that his dog has no faults, or too few to mention. No matter how many times an owner reads the breed standard, he cannot find any faults in his aristocratic companion dog. If this sounds like you, and if you are considering entering your Field Spaniel in a dog show, here are some basic questions to ask yourself:

- Did you purchase a "show-quality" puppy from the breeder?
- Is your puppy at least six months of age?
- Does the puppy exhibit correct show type for his breed?
- Does your puppy have any disqualifying faults?
- Is your Field Spaniel registered with the American Kennel Club?
- How much time do you have to devote to training, grooming, conditioning and exhibiting your dog?
- Do you understand the rules and regulations of a dog show?
- Do you have time to learn how to show your dog properly?
- Do you have the financial resources to invest in showing your dog?
- Will you show the dog yourself or hire a professional handler?
- Do you have a vehicle that can accommodate your weekend trips to the dog shows?

Success in the show ring requires more than a pretty face, a waggy tail and a pocketful of liver. Even though dog shows can be exciting and enjoyable, the sport of conformation makes great demands on the exhibitors and the dogs. Winning exhibitors live for their dogs, devoting time and money to their dogs' presentation, conditioning and training. Very few novices, even those with good dogs, will find themselves in the winners' circle, though it does happen. Don't be disheartened, though. Every exhibitor began as a novice and worked his way up to the Group ring. It's the "working your way up" part that you must keep in mind.

Assuming that you have purchased a puppy of the correct

type and quality for showing, let's begin to examine the world of showing and what's required to get started. Although the entry fee into a dog show is nominal, there are lots of other hidden costs involved with "finishing" your Field Spaniel, that is, making him a champion. Things like equipment, travel, training and conditioning all cost money. A more serious campaign will include fees for a professional handler, boarding, cross-country travel and advertising. Top-winning show dogs can represent a very considerable investment—over $100,000 has been spent in campaigning some dogs. (The investment can be less, of course, for owners who don't use professional handlers.)

Many owners, on the other hand, enter their "average" Field Spaniels in dog shows for the fun and enjoyment of it. Dog showing makes an absorbing hobby, with many rewards for dogs and owners alike. If you're having fun, meeting other people who share your interests and enjoying the overall experience, you likely will catch the "bug." Once the dog-show bug bites, its effects can last a lifetime; it's certainly much better than a deer tick! Soon you will be envisioning yourself in the center ring at the Westminster Kennel Club Dog Show in New York City, competing for the prestigious Best in Show cup. This magical dog show is televised annually from Madison Square Garden, and the victorious dog becomes a celebrity overnight.

AKC CONFORMATION-SHOW BASICS

Visiting a dog show as a spectator is a great place to start. Pick up the show catalog to find out what time your breed is being shown, who is judging the breed and in which ring the classes will be held. To start, Field Spaniels compete against other Field Spaniels, and the winner is selected as Best of Breed by the judge. This is the procedure for each breed. At a group show, all of the Best of Breed winners go on to compete for Group One (first place) in their respective groups. For example, all Best of Breed winners in a given group compete against each other;

BECOMING A CHAMPION

An official AKC championship of record requires that a dog accumulate 15 points under three different judges, including two "majors" under different judges. Points are awarded based on the number of dogs entered into competition, varying from breed to breed and place to place. A win of three, four or five points is considered a "major." The AKC annually assigns a schedule of points to adjust for variations that accompany a breed's popularity and the population of a given area.

AKC GROUPS

For showing purposes, the American Kennel Club divides its recognized breeds into seven groups: Sporting Dogs, Hounds, Working Dogs, Terriers, Toys, Non-Sporting Dogs and Herding Dogs.

this is done for all seven groups. The Field Spaniel competes in the Sporting Group. Finally, all seven group winners go head to head in the ring for the Best in Show award.

What most spectators don't understand is the basic idea of conformation. A dog show is often referred as a "conformation" show. This means that the judge should decide how each dog stacks up (conforms) to the breed standard for his given breed: how well does this Field Spaniel conform to the ideal representative detailed in the standard? Ideally, this is what happens. In reality, however, this ideal often gets slighted as the judge compares Field Spaniel #1 to Field Spaniel #2. Again, the ideal is that each dog is judged based on his merits in comparison to his breed standard, not in comparison to the other dogs in the ring. It is easier for judges to compare dogs of the same breed to decide which they think is the better specimen; in the Group and Best in Show rings, however, it is very difficult to compare one breed to another, like apples to oranges. Thus the dog's conformation to the breed standard—not to mention advertising dollars and good handling—is essential to success in conformation shows. The dog described in the standard (the standard for each AKC breed is written and approved by the breed's national

The line-up of Field Spaniels is "stacked" (standing) and ready for the judge's review in the breed ring.

parent club and then submitted to the AKC for approval) is the perfect dog of that breed, and breeders keep their eye on the standard when they choose which dogs to breed, hoping to get closer and closer to the ideal with each litter.

Another good first step for the novice is to join a dog club. You will be astonished by the many and different kinds of dog clubs in the country, with about 5,000 clubs holding events every year. Most clubs require that prospective new members present two letters of recommendation from existing members. Perhaps you've made some friends visiting a show held by a particular club and you would like to join that club. Dog clubs may specialize in a single breed, like a regional Field Spaniel club, or in a specific pursuit, such as obedience, tracking or hunting tests. There are all-breed clubs for all dog enthusiasts; they sponsor special training days, seminars on topics like grooming or handling or lectures on breeding or canine genetics. There are also clubs that specialize in certain types of dogs, like hunting dogs, herding dogs, companion dogs, etc. For more information about dog clubs in your area, contact the AKC at www.akc.org on the Internet or write them at their Raleigh, NC address.

A parent club is the national organization, sanctioned by the AKC, which promotes and safeguards its breed in the country. The parent club for the Field Spaniel, the Field Spaniel Society of America, Inc., was formed in 1978. The parent club holds an annual national specialty show, usually in a different city each year, in which many of the country's top dogs, handlers and breeders gather to compete. At a specialty show, only members of a single breed are invited to participate. There are also group specialties, in which all members of a group are invited. The FSSA also holds special events for hunting, tracking, obedi-

FIVE CLASSES AT SHOWS

At most AKC all-breed shows, there are five regular classes offered: Puppy, Novice, Bred-by-Exhibitor, American-bred and Open. The Puppy Class is usually divided as 6 to 9 months of age and 9 to 12 months of age. When deciding in which class to enter your dog, whether male or female, you must carefully check the show schedule to make sure that you have selected the right class. Depending on the age of the dog, previous first-place wins and the sex of the dog, you must make the best choice. It is possible to enter a one-year-old dog who has not won sufficient first places in any of the non-Puppy Classes, though the competition is more intense the further you progress from the Puppy Class.

The Field Spaniel's gait reveals the quality of its construction to the judge.

ence and agility, for titles and just for fun. Contact the FSSA online at http://clubs.akc.org/fssa.

OTHER TYPES OF COMPETITION

In addition to conformation shows, the AKC holds a variety of other competitive events. Obedience trials, agility trials and tracking trials are open to all breeds, while hunting tests, field trials, lure coursing, herding tests and trials, earthdog tests and coonhound events are limited to specific breeds or groups of breeds. The Junior Showmanship program is offered to aspiring young handlers and their dogs, and the Canine Good Citizen® Program is an all-around good-behavior test open to all dogs, pure-bred and mixed. Field Spaniels have demonstrated superior ability in all areas of competition for which they are eligible.

Obedience Trials

Mrs. Helen Whitehouse Walker, a Standard Poodle fancier, can be credited with introducing obedience trials to the United States. In the 1930s she designed a series of exercises based on those of the Associated Sheep, Police, Army Dog Society of Great Britain. These exercises were intended to evaluate the working relationship between dog and owner. Since those early days of the sport in the US, obedience trials have grown more and more popular, and now more than 2,000 trials each year attract over 100,000 dogs and their owners. Any dog registered with the AKC, regardless of neutering or other disqualifications that would preclude entry in conformation competition, can participate in obedience trials.

There are three levels of difficulty in obedience competition. The first (and easiest) level is the Novice, in which dogs can earn the Companion Dog (CD) title. The intermediate level is the Open level, in which the Companion Dog Excellent (CDX) title is awarded. The advanced level is the Utility level, in which dogs compete for the Utility Dog (UD) title. Classes at each level are further divided into "A" and "B," with "A" for beginners and "B" for those with more experience. In order to win a title at a given level, a dog must earn three "legs." A "leg" is accomplished when a dog scores 170 or higher (200 is a perfect score). The scoring system gets a little trickier when you understand that a dog must score more than 50% of the points available for each exercise in order to actually earn the points. Available points for each exercise range between 20 and 40.

A dog must complete different exercises at each level of obedience. The Novice exercises are the easiest, with the Open and finally the Utility levels progressing in difficulty. Examples of Novice exercises are on- and off-lead heeling, a figure-8 pattern, performing a recall (or come), long sit and long down and standing for examination. In the Open level, the Novice-level exercises are required again, but this time without a leash and for longer durations. In addition, the dog must clear a broad jump, retrieve over a jump and drop on recall. In the Utility level, the exercises are quite difficult, including executing basic commands based on hand signals, following a complex heeling pattern, locating articles based on scent discrimination and completing jumps at the handler's direction.

Once he's earned the UD title, a dog can go on to win the prestigious title of Utility Dog Excellent (UDX) by winning "legs" in ten shows. Additionally, Utility Dogs who win "legs" in Open B and Utility B earn points toward the lofty title of Obedience Trial Champion (OTCh.). Established in 1977 by the AKC, this title requires a dog to earn 100 points as well as three first places in a combination of Open B and Utility B classes under three different judges. The first Field Spaniel to achieve the Obedience Trial Champion title was Ch. OTCh. Calico's Lil Deuce Coupe UDX. The "brass ring" of obedience competition is the AKC's National Obedience Invitational. This is an exclusive competition for only the cream of the obedience crop. In order to qualify for the invitational, a dog must be ranked in either the top 25 all-breeds in obedience or in the

Race is the first Champion Tracker in the breed, a national specialty winner and a quality sire. He also competed with the author's daughter Kylie, shown here, in Junior Showmanship.

top 3 for his breed in obedience. The title at stake here is that of National Obedience Champion (NOC).

Rally Obedience

In 2005 the AKC began a new program called rally obedience, and soon this exciting obedience spin-off began sweeping the US. This is a less formal activity than traditional obedience competition, and titles are awarded. In fact, Field Spaniel Ch. Winters' Hopes and Prayers VCD1, RN earned the first rally title just a few short weeks after the title became available. There are four levels of competition: Novice, Advanced, Excellent and Advanced/Excellent. The dog and handler do a series of exercises designed by the judge and are timed. The handlers are encouraged to talk to their dogs as they work through the course. The judge evaluates each team on how well it executes one continuous performance over the whole course.

The team works on its own as soon as the judge gives the order to begin. Handlers develop their own styles in working with their dogs, using a combination of body language and hand signals as well as verbal commands. Faster and more accurate performances are desirable, though each team must work at its own pace. Signs are set up around the ring to indicate which exercise (or combination of exercises) is required. Working closely around the course, the team heels from one sign to the next, performing the various exercises. There are 50 exercises to choose from, varying in complexity and difficulty.

The dogs love this sport and it shows in their animation and

CANINE GOOD CITIZEN® PROGRAM

Have you ever considered getting your dog "certified"? The AKC's Canine Good Citizen® Program affords your dog just that opportunity. Your dog shows that he is a well-behaved canine citizen, using the basic training and good manners you have taught him, by taking a series of ten tests that illustrate that he can behave properly at home, in a public place and around other dogs. The tests are administered by participating dog clubs, colleges, 4-H clubs, Scouts and other community groups and are open to all pure-bred and mixed-breed dogs. Upon passing the ten tests, the suffix CGC is then applied to your dog's name.

The ten tests are: 1. Accepting a friendly stranger; 2. Sitting politely for petting; 3. Appearance and grooming; 4. Walking on a lead; 5. Walking through a group of people; 6. Sit, down and stay on command; 7. Coming when called; 8. Meeting another dog; 9. Calm reaction to distractions; 10. Separation from owner.

energy. Many of the dogs who participate in obedience or agility also do well in rally. While most of the first rally titles have gone to seasoned obedience dogs, it's encouraging that some newcomers have also earned awards. Rally is a good way for a beginner to start out in obedience, and we hope that it will become a stepping stone to the obedience world and that we will see many more dogs and owners coming into the ring.

Agility Trials

Agility trials became sanctioned by the AKC in August 1994, when the first licensed agility trials were held. Since that time, agility certainly has grown in popularity by leaps and bounds, literally! The AKC allows all registered breeds (including Miscellaneous Class breeds) to participate, providing the dog is 12 months of age or older. Agility is designed so that the handler demonstrates how well the dog can work at his side. The handler directs his dog through, over, under and around an obstacle course that includes jumps, tires, the dog walk, weave poles, pipe tunnels, collapsed tunnels and more. While working his way through the course, the dog must keep one eye and ear on the handler and the rest of his body on the course. The handler runs along with the dog, giving verbal and hand signals to guide the dog through the course.

Field Spaniels are enthusiastic competitors and usually do well in agility trials.

The first organization to promote agility trials in the US was the United States Dog Agility Association, Inc. (USDAA). Established in 1986, the USDAA sparked the formation of many member clubs around the country. To participate in USDAA trials, dogs must be at least 18 months of age. The USDAA and AKC both offer titles to winning dogs, although the exercises and requirements of the two organizations differ. At present, the prestigious AKC Master Agility Champion title has yet to be achieved by a Field Spaniel; however, Ch. Bitterblue's Windward Tiller TDX, AX, AXJ has been most notably blazing pathways in the agility ring.

Agility trials are a great way to keep your dog active, and they will keep you running, too! You should join a local agility club to

The impressively titled Ch. Calico's Moving Picture MH, CDX, RN, WDX was the first Field Spaniel to earn a conformation championship and a Master Hunter title.

learn more about the sport. These clubs offer sessions in which you can introduce your dog to the various obstacles as well as training classes to prepare him for competition. In no time, your dog will be climbing A-frames, crossing the dog walk and flying over hurdles, all with you right beside him. Your heart will leap every time your dog jumps through the hoop—and you'll be having just as much (if not more) fun!

Tracking

Tracking tests are exciting ways to test your Field Spaniel's instinctive scenting ability on a competitive level. All dogs have a nose, and all breeds are welcome in tracking tests. The first AKC-licensed tracking test took place in 1937 as part of the Utility level at an obedience trial, and thus competitive tracking was officially begun. The first title, Tracking Dog (TD), was offered in 1947, ten years after the first official tracking test. It was not until 1980 that the AKC added the title Tracking Dog Excellent (TDX), which was followed by the title Variable Surface Tracking (VST) in 1995. Champion Tracker (CT) is awarded to a dog who has earned all three of those titles. The first Field Spaniel to acheive the CT title was Ch. CT Calico's Hot Pursuit Del Prado.

The TD level is the first and most basic level in tracking, progressing in difficulty to the TDX and then the VST. A dog must follow a track laid by a human 30 to 120 minutes prior in order to earn the TD title. The track is about 500 yards long and contains up to 5 directional changes. At the next level, the TDX, the dog must follow a 3- to 5-hour-old track over a course that is up to 1,000 yards long and has up to 7 directional changes. In the most difficult level, the VST, the track is up to 5 hours old and located in an urban setting.

Hunting Tests

Though the Field Spaniel is not eligible to run in AKC field trials, the AKC offers a hunting-test program in which Fields can participate and earn titles. Hunting tests are not competitive like field trials, and participating dogs are judged against a standard, as in a conformation show. The intent of hunting tests is to test the dog's ability in a simulated hunting scenario.

The AKC instituted its hunting tests in June 1985; since then, their popularity has grown tremendously. The AKC offers three titles at hunting tests, Junior Hunter (JH), Senior Hunter (SH) and Master Hunter (MH). Each title requires that the dog earn qualifying "legs" at the tests: the JH requiring four; the SH, five; and the MH, six. The first Master Hunter in the Field Spaniel breed was Calico's Chantilly Lace MH. In addition to the AKC, the United Kennel Club (www.ukcdogs.com) offers hunting tests through its affiliate club, the Hunting Retriever Club, Inc., which began the tests in 1984.

Ch. Woodrun's Yesterday UD, JH, WD (a.k.a. "Keeper") is a bitch known for her beautiful head and tremendous bird drive—and has the titles to prove it!

HRC HUNT TESTS

The most realistic hunt-test program in North America is that of the Hunting Retriever Club (HRC, found at www.hrc-ukc.com), a United Kennel Club (UKC) affiliate. The Hunting Retriever Club provides the opportunity for participants to hunt with their dogs in front of a judge; any sporting-breed dog is eligible to participate. Specifically, the tests are true hunting scenarios in which handlers actually use guns. Judges are qualified HRC members who own, have trained and have passed their dogs in the level that they are judging. There are 116 HRC member clubs with over 8,000 individual members. These folks take hunting seriously and have fun as well.

Judges create tests for actual hunting situations using realistic hunting distances, cover and terrain. The HRC program tests dogs against a written standard instead of against each other. Three categories, Started, Seasoned and Finished, are offered at each hunt test. The Natural Ability Test (NAT) and field trial rules were developed directly from the rules of European trials, in which the dog must hunt for the foot hunter.

INDEX

*Page numbers in **boldface** indicate illustrations.*

My Field Spaniel

PUT YOUR PUPPY'S FIRST PICTURE HERE

Dog's Name ______________________________

Date ______________ Photographer ______________________